Instant Session Plans
for
Essential Life Skills:
Learning and Development

Robin Dynes

Russell House Publishing

First published in 2009 by:
Russell House Publishing Ltd.
4 St. George's House
Uplyme Road
Lyme Regis
Dorset DT7 3LS

Tel: 01297-443948
Fax: 01297-442722
e-mail: help@russellhouse.co.uk
www.russellhouse.co.uk

© Robin Dynes

British Library Cataloguing-in-publication Data:
A catalogue record for this book is available from the British Library.

ISBN: 978-1-905541-41-6

Typeset by TW Typesetting, Plymouth, Devon

Printed by Ashford Press, Southampton

About Russell House Publishing

Russell House Publishing aims to publish innovative and valuable materials to help managers, practitioners, trainers, educators and students.

Our full catalogue covers: social policy, working with young people, helping children and families, care of older people, social care, combating social exclusion, revitalising communities and working with offenders.

Full details can be found at www.russellhouse.co.uk and we are pleased to send out information to you by post. Our contact details are on this page.

We are always keen to receive feedback on publications and new ideas for future projects.

Contents

Photocopying permission for the use of the handouts

1. Permission to photocopy the handouts is only given to **individuals or organisations who have bought a copy of the book** and then only for distribution at the local level within their organisation. The price of this book has deliberately been kept affordable to smaller organisations. It is therefore expected that, as a matter of honour, larger organisations – for example national or countywide statutory or voluntary organisations – who might want to use the photocopiable material in numerous locations, will buy a copy of the book for use in each locality where they are using the material.
2. If a **trainer or an educational organisation** wants to copy and distribute these handouts to assist their work with clients in organisations where they are training, it is expected that they will buy a copy of the book for each organisation where they undertake such training and – in line with the principles set out in point 1 (above) – a copy for each locality when they are training in a large organisation at multiple locations. This expectation is based on respect for the author's copyright and the view that providing manuals in this way will add to the benefits delivered in the training. The publisher and author therefore seek trainers' active support in this matter.
3. Under no circumstances should anyone sell photocopied material from this book without the express permission of the publisher.

If in doubt, anyone wanting to make photocopies should contact the publisher, via email at help@russellhouse.co.uk.

Other photocopying permission

Anyone wishing to copy all or part of the handouts *in any context other than set out here* should first seek permission in the usual way:

- either via Russell House Publishing
- or via the Copyright Licensing Agency.

Anyone wishing to copy any other part of this book in any context, beyond normal fair trading guidelines, should first seek permission in the usual way:

- either via Russell House Publishing
- or via the Copyright Licensing Agency.

Electronic supply of the handouts

A PDF of the approximately 80 pages of this manual, on which the handouts appear, is available free, by email from RHP, to purchasers of the book who complete and return the licence request at the end of the book.

Please note that anyone who is reading this in a copy of the book from which the tear-out coupon has been removed would need to buy a new copy of the book in order to be able to apply for the electronic materials.

The following terms and conditions for use of the electronic materials apply in all cases:

Terms and conditions for use of handouts from Instant Session Plans for Essential Life Skills: Learning and Development

1. Buying a copy of *Instant Session Plans for Essential Life Skills: Learning and Development* and completing the form at the back of this book gives the individual who signs the form permission to use the materials in the PDF that will be sent from RHP for their own use only.
2. The hard copies that they then print from the PDF are subject to the same permissions and restrictions that are set out in the 'photocopying permission' section at the front of this book.
3. Under no circumstances should they forward or copy the electronic materials to anyone else.
4. If the person who signs this form wants a licence to be granted for wider use of the electronic materials within their organisation, network or client base, they must make a request directly to RHP fully detailing the proposed use. All requests will be reviewed on their own merits.
   - If the request is made when submitting this form to RHP, the request should be made in writing and should accompany this form.
   - If the request is made later, it should be made in an email sent to help@russellhouse.co.uk, and should not only fully detail the proposed use, but also give the details of the person whose name and contact details were on the original application form.

RHP and the author expect this honour system to be followed respectfully, by individuals and organisations whom we in turn respect. RHP will act to protect authors' copyright if they become aware of it being infringed.

Introduction

What are essential life skills?

Essential life skills are the wide range of acquirable habits and skills we all use to manage and cope with life. Explicitly, managing the events and situations we face daily, being able to acknowledge and have our personal needs met and being able to achieve our ambitions. Developing these skills enables us to become more effective in how we:

- solve problems
- deal with stress
- look after ourselves and maintain good health
- manage day-to-day affairs
- communicate with others
- think about ourselves
- live our lives
- cope with life.

Why 'Instant Session Plans'?

They are a 'toolkit' resource which has been developed from my experience over 25 years of working with a wide range of different types of groups in different environments. The settings have included psychiatric hospitals, day centres, special schools, schools and adult learning. The diverse backgrounds of groups formed have included mental ill health, physical disabilities, learning disabilities, alcohol and drug addiction, offender supervision, students leaving school or in transition from school to adult learning and adults preparing to return to work after a long absence.

Working with a wide range of different types of groups has needed resource material that is both 'flexible' and 'adaptable' for use with diverse needs. The material 'flexibility' has also had to be suitable for colleagues to use to lead groups and courses they have been facilitating.

The bank of resources has been necessary to meet the demand, frequently at short notice, to provide appropriate material for the groups. Also, when facilitating a group, often it quickly becomes apparent that a carefully planned programme will not meet some of the needs which are emerging. Having a bank of 'Instant Session Plans' to hand has enabled 'instant' and timely changes to programme sessions to meet that need and respond to the specific requirements of group members.

What is offered?

Instant Session Plans for Essential Life Skills – Learning and Development is the third volume in a series of 'Instant Session Plan' resource books. The first and second books were *Instant Session Plans for Essential Life Skills – Self-Management and Instant Session Plans for Essential Life Skills – Learning and Development.* The fourth book planned is *Instant Session Plans for Essential Life Skills – Relationships.*

The volumes bring together the material developed and will be indispensable for busy group facilitators working in hospitals, day or youth centres, adult learning, schools and other environments with youths or adults who need to develop essential life skills. The series is aimed at busy social, youth, probation, care and health workers, teachers or anyone working with groups that require 'instant' or ready made sessions.

The sessions are invaluable to:

- The less experienced practitioner.
- The more experienced group leader who requires fresh supplementary resources to complement their existing material.
- Anyone who needs adaptable and flexible material to put together packages to meet the needs of particular groups or individuals.
- Group facilitators who want material from which to select to meet particular requirements.
- Anyone wanting to set up an essential life skills club.

Each session contains handouts that can be photocopied and clear step-by-step instructions for the group leader. The sessions can be used with adults or teenagers in a wide variety of environments.

The activities involve participants working as a group, on their own, in pairs and in sub-groups. Discussion and practical exercises are related to group members' everyday experiences to make the learning and development both dynamic and enjoyable.

How to use this book

Instant Sessions Plans for Essential Life Skills – Learning and Development contains 42 sessions. This includes an introduction session to use when starting to work on essential life skills with a new group and a session to bring the group to an end. Forty sessions are divided into ten different essential life skill topics:

- Unlocking Your Potential
- Learning to Learn
- Becoming Self-motivated
- Self-coaching
- Emotional Development
- Harnessing Creativity
- Life Management Skills
- Understanding Yourself
- Learning From Experience
- Planning for Your Future

Each topic section contains four sessions. Each session is complete and consists of:

- Aims for the session.
- Any preparation required. (This is kept to a minimum – but facilitators do need to familiarise themselves with the notes and handouts supplied before beginning a session.)
- Notes for the activities which incorporate: approximate timings, an introduction to the topic, development activities for the session, a closure activity and homework. Skills practice, linked to personal experience and needs, are incorporated into the activities and homework.
- One or more handouts for each session.

The handouts are placed with the notes to make life easier for the facilitator, also to make the book 'user-friendly' and easy to use.

Built in flexibility

Each session can be used on its own, as a supplement to other material or several sessions chosen to meet particular needs. For example, if forming a group with needs identified such as:

- Learning to learn
- Becoming self-motivated
- Emotional development
- Learning from experience
- Planning for your future

Sessions can be chosen from each of these sections to meet the identified need and put together to make a ten week course.

The various sections supplement and support each other. For example, a session or two from 'Learning to Learn' may well meet an identified need when the main aim for a particular group is 'Planning for Your Future'. These sessions can then be used as part of the programme for a 'planning for your future' group. Many of the sessions and activities, with some adaptation, can also be used when working with individuals.

Do the session plans need to be used as they are laid out? No, shorten them by selecting some components, split them over two sessions or add additions of your own. Adapt them and change teaching methods to suit particular needs or so that participants feel comfortable with what you are presenting. For example: if anyone has difficulty reading or writing, have someone available to pair them with who will go through the handouts verbally with them and write down their answers. Alternatively, they could record the questions and answers on a tape for them to play back at home. Answers could also be drawn rather than written. Learning requirements can be solved in different ways to suit the needs of particular individuals. Adapting this sort of flexible attitude to the sessions is necessary when working with different types of groups.

This type of flexibility will also be built into future volumes, so they can be used in conjunction with each other and build into an extensive resource covering a wide range of topics and needs.

Timing

Each session lasts for about one hour when working with groups of 6–10 people. Time allowances will need to be made for:

- larger groups
- the abilities of the group members
- different types of groups

If running a series of sessions it is recommended that additional time is allowed to enable group members to give feedback on their progress with the homework from the previous session – about 10–15 minutes is usually adequate.

Setting up a group

Attention to detail when setting up a group will help ensure it is a success. How you go about the process will be influenced by the circumstances and demands of the setting you work in – school, youth centre, adult learning, day centre, hospital or offender supervision. Here is a list of some of the things you will need to think about:

- *Establishing need.* It is necessary to gather evidence that a group of the type you propose is needed. As well as establishing need, evidence provides accountability to authorities, parents, etc. In some settings the need may be established and you are given the task of organising the group
- *Writing a proposal.* This should detail what you are going to do and how you are going to do it. The proposal will enable you to answer any questions you may be asked by colleagues referring to the group, as well as potential group members. It is also essential for obtaining necessary permissions from parents or guardians. The proposal should include details such as:
  – The group aims.
  – Who the group is for.
  – What needs will be met.
  – Topics to be covered.
  – How group members are to be selected.
  – When and where the group will meet.
  – What techniques will be used.
  – How confidentiality boundaries will be handled.
  – What is to be put in place for referred members who are not selected.
  – Any special precautions needed because of the client group.
  – How success for each participant will be measured.
  – What follow up will be provided.
  – What happens to evaluation data and who will have access to it.
  – What problems you expect to encounter at different stages and how these will be dealt with.
- *Recruiting group members.* How this happens depends on the setting. In some settings key workers, social workers or other staff may refer clients to the group, or the group may need to be advertised. If you are targeting a particular type of client – such as people with

mental health problems or young people – you will need to make that clear in any advertising material.

- *Obtaining consent.* Settings such as schools or day centres will have set procedures for obtaining any necessary consent from parents or guardians. Follow that procedure.
- *Pre-group interviews.* The purpose of pre-group interviews is to provide information to possible participants, obtain their consent, ensure their commitment and obtain information from them to help you in the selection process. It is important that the interviewee is given full information about the group, as detailed in your group proposal.

You will also need to find out from them what their expectations are, why they want to take part and if there are any influences which could make it difficult for them at this time. For example, going through a crisis, acute anxiety, depression or other reasons. Ensure they understand that they may experience some feelings of discomfort at times when working through difficulties and making changes. Establish if there are any special needs or discrimination issues that will need to be addressed, such as lack of ability to read and write, learning disability, hearing impairment, cultural requirements, etc.

Summarise and ask questions throughout the interview to ensure that the person understands the information you are giving and what will be expected from them. At the end of the interview they should be able to make an informed decision about committing themselves to the group. The information you obtain should enable you to select group members who will benefit most from the sessions and help you to decide:

- The level at which to pitch the course.
- What language level to use.
- What support is needed for individuals.
- What teaching methods to use.
- What teaching aids will be most useful.
- What will be required to avoid discrimination.

- *Selecting group members.* Avoid selecting group members who:

  - All have the same negative behaviours (if everyone has the same difficulty there will be no positive models to learn from).
  - Have extreme differences in abilities.
  - Are abusive verbally or physically.
  - Are undergoing a crisis (unless the group is in response to that crisis).

Avoid people feeling rejected if they are not chosen by:

  - Making it clear in any advertising or preliminary discussions that not everyone may be included.
  - Planning a group at a later date to meet the needs of those who cannot be included.
  - Explaining why they have not been selected.
  - Referring them to more appropriate services such as individual counselling.

Avoiding discrimination

All authorities (and most settings) have anti-discrimination policies that include disability, race and ethnicity, gender, sexual orientation, religion and belief and age. Authorities have a duty to enforce and promote these policies. It is essential that all group facilitators – whatever the setting – also actively enforce and promote anti-discriminatory practice. Examples of options to consider include:

- Putting discrimination on the group agenda. This can be accomplished as part of the group agreeing 'ground rules' in the first session. For example, a rule might be, 'No discriminating language or behaviour' or 'Respecting everyone's right to be in, and contribute to, the group'. Explain that, while other rules are negotiable, this is not. This then gives you or anyone else in the group a mandate to confront any behaviour, should it emerge.
- Taking steps to ensure that the environment in which the group meets is inclusive. Do the images displayed on the walls provoke an inclusive atmosphere?
- Ensuring that content, method of delivery, language and style adopted are appropriate to the group membership. Be open to criticism and feedback from group members.
- Widening the group catchment area so that the group membership can be balanced. For example, other teams or day centres might have people with similar needs and be willing to support the group in a partnership venture.
- Trying to compensate for disadvantages. You may find yourself working with a group that has been formed without your input – you have no say in the membership. If there is only one black or gay member in the group could they obtain one-to-one support from a black or gay member of staff? Perhaps you could enlist a co-worker who is black or gay?
- Arranging for an appropriate group supervisor who represents the minority in the group. Alternatively, invite someone to act as a group consultant who is qualified to understand and represent the minority viewpoint.
- Running a group to meet specific requirements. For example, a women or men only group. This might equally apply to race and ethnicity, religion and belief, disability, sexual orientation or age, particularly when issues might arise that make disclosure and discussion difficult in a mixed group.

Health and safety

You will need to comply with and actively enforce the policy of the setting in which you are working. For example, if working in an Adult Learning setting there will be a risk assessment for the activity, the building, classroom and equipment you are using. There will also be an additional risk assessment – sometimes called a risk and support plan – for individual learners who, because of their special needs, require one. This might be because of sight impairment, panic attacks, medical conditions, behavioural difficulties etc. The plan will detail action to be taken to reduce any risks – emotional or physical – to that learner or other people to an acceptable level. It is essential that the learner, their carer, social or health worker, the group facilitator and any relevant others are all involved in deciding and agreeing the contents of that plan.

Preparing for role-play

The use of exercises and role-play is a part of any essential life skills course. Role-play enables participants to focus on their behaviour, its effect on other people and to explore different approaches to difficult situations and practice them within a safe environment. Everyone experiences anxieties about participating in them – especially if being observed by other people.

Allay fears by:

- Explaining what role-plays and exercises are about. Group members often think that role-play is a form of acting. It is not; it may be reliving a situation, trying out new ways of dealing with particular problems within a safe environment or learning a new skill. Emphasise that it enables them to make mistakes and learn from them. Point out that while doing role-play they may experience some of the feelings and inhibitions generated in real life.

Obtaining feedback from observers and discussing observations helps them:

  - Learn about the effects their reactions and behaviour has on others.
  - Explore how they can deal with situations or problems more effectively.
  - Improve their performance when learning new skills.

- Giving the group members opportunity to share their anxieties about role-play or exercises.

The importance of homework

Homework is integral to the sessions for a number of reasons:

- It accelerates progress and generalises newly acquired skills to real situations.
- Participants gain confidence from doing things on their own without the support of a facilitator. They begin to realise they can solve problems and cope with situations in a variety of different environments and manage on their own.
- It enhances confidence in the facilitator and the group when they are able to work through homework difficulties in feedback sessions.
- It tests the validity of the development process.
- It teaches discipline and helps develop the ability to follow through and work hard to achieve goals.
- It provides direction and structure to the development process. Starting a session with feedback and ending with new homework gives a message that the sessions are about making changes.

If group members are particularly vulnerable or anxious it can be helpful to avoid using the word 'homework' by calling it 'practice'. This has the effect of lowering anxiety, indicates that failure is OK and that performing the task perfectly is not required or necessary.

Organising the sessions

In most of the sessions participants will spend time working on their own, in pairs, in sub-groups or as a group. To accommodate this, a certain amount of room reorganisation may be needed.

If possible, arrange the room to enable group members working in pairs or sub-groups to avoid disturbing each other. If this is not possible, individuals can work with the person next to them on the left or right. When there are an uneven number of participants, most of the pairing activities can be completed by three people.

As far as possible, vary the pairs and groups, so that participants do not always work with the same people. It can be useful, for example, to mix more confident group members with those who are more reticent in a sub-group so that they can help each other.

The advantage of working in pairs and sub-groups is that it gives everyone a chance to speak in a non-threatening environment – with fellow participants rather than in front of the facilitator and the whole group. Participants learn from each other in a natural way that simulates the real world and avoids the constraints of a formal group. It can be useful, especially if these types of activities are new to people, to explain the advantages of working in this way to encourage them to participate as much as they can.

The role of the facilitator while these activities are taking place is to encourage communication by walking round the room, pausing briefly with each pair or sub-group and provide help and encouragement as needed. If discussing difficulties you have picked up on with the whole group later, avoid stating who had the difficulty as this could have a discouraging effect.

Finally

Experience has taught me that:

- Being flexible.
- Creating a warm and welcoming atmosphere.
- Listening to what people say and showing that I have listened to them.
- Being willing to accept criticism and feedback.
- Relaxing and enjoying the sessions . . .

are essential to make the sessions successful. I wish you joy in using the books.

Introduction Session for Essential Life Skills

Aims

- To welcome everyone.
- To help group members get to know each other.
- To agree ground rules.
- To make group members aware of the course contents.
- To clarify what will be expected from everyone.
- To evaluate the starting point for each person.

Preparation

Have a flipchart, magic markers and photocopies of the handout available.

Introduction (15 minutes)

Welcome everyone. State the aims for the course you are presenting and how this will be achieved. For example:

Aim: to enable you to cope with life situations.

by: developing your life skills.

through: sharing information, learning from personal experience, discussion and exercise.

This can be written on a flip chart and displayed on a wall for each session that you choose to run.

Next, inform the participants about any practical arrangements such as:

- Fire procedures.
- Location of toilets.
- Refreshments.
- Breaks.
- Seating arrangements.
- Length of sessions, how many and what will be covered.
- The structure of sessions.
- Homework.
- The use of discussion, role play, exercises and feedback.

When complete state the aims for this session.

Activity (10 minutes)

As an icebreaker and a means of introducing people to each other ask group members to think of someone who has influenced them in some way. This might be a friend, a grandparent, a teacher, a colleague or a famous person they admire or dislike. Invite them to state their name, who and how that person has influenced them. The exercise also prepares people to start making disclosures and build trust.

Activity (15 minutes)

Lead a discussion with participants about rules they would like the group to follow. Use a flip chart to record any agreed guidelines and expectations. Consider:

- Confidentiality
- Everyone's right to express their opinion and have it respected
- How they will support each other
- Being non-judgmental
- Commitment to completing homework
- Not interrupting each other
- Turning up on time
- How they will challenge and be willing to be challenged
- Valuing and listening to each others contribution

Explain that as sessions progress if any issues develop they might like to add new rules to deal with them. It is often helpful to review the rules part way through the course or if there are any infringements to remind people about what has been agreed. The guidelines can also be displayed at each session.

Activity (10 minutes)

Divide the participants into sub groups or, if the group is small, into pairs. Ask them to discuss why they are attending the course and what they want from it. After about five minutes, bring everyone back together and have each person state why they are attending. This might include statements like:

- 'I keep making the same mistakes. How do I learn and move on?'
- 'I didn't enjoy learning at school. I would like to know how to improve my ability to learn.'
- 'I start things but hardly ever complete them. I want to know how to keep myself motivated.'

Record their expectations on a flipchart. Inform participants that you will keep the sheet to have available for the final session to find out if their expectations have been met.

Closure (5 minutes)

Invite questions about what has been agreed and for future sessions. Clarify any misunderstandings and ask each person, in turn, to state how they feel. If anyone feels uncomfortable or anxious, tactfully try to find the out reason for their discomfort and allay any fears.

Homework (5 minutes)

Remind everyone of both your own and group members' expectations. Give out Handout 1 with appropriate chosen topics (Anger Management, Assertiveness etc.) filled in. Ask participants to self-assess themselves in the topics chosen for the course and bring them back for the next session. Explain that you will keep these safe until the course has been completed when you will ask them to complete a second chart to establish what, if any, improvement has taken place.

Introduction to Essential Life Skills: Handout 1

Self-rating chart

Name: _____   Date: _____

Rate your ability in the following areas:	Poor				Good
	1	2	3	4	5
	1	2	3	4	5
	1	2	3	4	5
	1	2	3	4	5
	1	2	3	4	5
	1	2	3	4	5
	1	2	3	4	5
	1	2	3	4	5
	1	2	3	4	5
	1	2	3	4	5
	1	2	3	4	5
	1	2	3	4	5

Unlocking Your Potential

- Identifying what is important
- Increasing positive energy
- Taking stock of your skills
- The freedom of boundaries

Identifying what is important

Aims

- To acknowledge what is important to you in your life.
- To recognise what you value and makes you feel good.
- To improve self-awareness.

Preparation

Have available copies of the handouts and a whiteboard or flipchart.

Introduction (10 minutes)

Explain the aims for the session. Ask each person in the group to think back to when they were younger or a child. They think of something that they wanted to do or be when they were older. After a moment for thought each person in turn, states what their dream was then.

Activity (5 minutes)

Write the title 'My Dream Life' up on a flipchart or whiteboard. Below the title draw some clouds as shown in Handout 1. Write in one cloud a dream of your own. This might be something like 'Spending more time with my daughter' or 'Write a novel'. Now ask group members to call out a dream they have. Examples might be:

- Open and run my own restaurant.
- Travel and see different cultures.
- Look after animals.
- Have lots of friends.
- Help other people in my spare time.
- Design clothes.

Write these up on the board as they are called out.

Activity (10 minutes)

Give out Handout 1 and ask each person to think about their dream life. What are their ambitions and hopes? What would they like to be doing? Ask them to think about different aspects of their lives such as:

- Work
- Social life
- Family life
- Relationships
- Where they are

They then write their ambitions and dreams down in the clouds.

Activity (10 minutes)

Lead a short discussion around how what they have written down indicates:

- What they value in life.
- What is important to them.
- How they want their future life to be.

Is anyone surprised about what they have written down? How often do people spend some time reflecting on how their life is and how they would like it to be? Is it important to have a dream? Why?

Activity (10 minutes)

Give out Handout 2 and, from what group members have learned about themselves in the previous activities, ask them to identify some of the things that are important to them in life. Give an example from your own life. Perhaps, that your dream was to be a tutor or social worker. What is important to you about this is being able to help other people.

Encourage participants to add other things which are important to them which are not listed on Handout 2.

Closure (10 minutes)

Ask each person, in turn, to make a statement completing the following:

A dream I have is . . .

What is important about this to me is . . .

Homework (5 minutes)

Ask each person to think of one thing they can do to take a first step towards fulfilling their dream. They then do it. This might be:

- Share their dream with their partner.
- Obtain information about something they want to do.
- Work out an action plan of how they are going to achieve it.
- Look at how they manage their time to ensure they have time to do what they want.

Identifying what is important: Handout 1

My dream life

Identifying what is important: Handout 2

Circle the number which indicates how important or unimportant each thing is to you. Add additional things you value and make you feel good which are not listed in the blank spaces

	Not important				Important
Independence	1	2	3	4	5
Status	1	2	3	4	5
Being creative and using my imagination	1	2	3	4	5
Risk taking	1	2	3	4	5
Helping other people	1	2	3	4	5
Friendships	1	2	3	4	5
Security	1	2	3	4	5
Challenge	1	2	3	4	5
Love	1	2	3	4	5
Learning	1	2	3	4	5
Routine	1	2	3	4	5
Physical challenge	1	2	3	4	5
Being respected	1	2	3	4	5
Having contact with other people	1	2	3	4	5
Family life	1	2	3	4	5
Responsibility	1	2	3	4	5
Having fun and enjoying life	1	2	3	4	5
Having pleasant surroundings	1	2	3	4	5

	1	2	3	4	5
Promotion	1	2	3	4	5
Personal values	1	2	3	4	5
Making decisions	1	2	3	4	5
Being able to do things when I want to	1	2	3	4	5
Having time alone	1	2	3	4	5
Recognition	1	2	3	4	5
Variety	1	2	3	4	5
	1	2	3	4	5
	1	2	3	4	5
	1	2	3	4	5
	1	2	3	4	5
	1	2	3	4	5
	1	2	3	4	5
	1	2	3	4	5

Increasing positive energy

Aims

- To explore barriers to positive energy.
- To discover personal energy drains.
- To develop a system to increase positive energy.

Preparation

Have available copies of the handout and a whiteboard or a flipchart.

Introduction (10 minutes)

Go through the aims for the session. Explain that most people have been conditioned to accept life as it is. They feel that they should make the best of their situation. They run around sorting out problems, dealing with things they would rather not deal with at all.

They may feel that they have no choice. It is easier and simpler to leave things as they are than attempt to make changes and risk trying something new. Putting up with things may feel uncomfortable but it would take too much effort to make changes. It is easier to put up with the discomfort.

Examples might be that your partner leaves a mess in the kitchen every time he does his/her hobby. You spend time clearing up after him/her. It is a drain on your energy but you tolerate it. Or, you may put up with your lack of confidence and this becomes a reason not to apply for a new job.

If it was only one thing it might not be so bad but most of us tolerate lots of things – both in ourselves and from others. Time is spent putting up with or managing situations that should not be there. We are conditioned to think of this as normal and we accept this damping down of our energy. The following exercises are aimed at examining and doing something about this drain on our energy.

Activity (15 minutes)

Write two heading on a flipchart or a whiteboard as shown below. Ask group members to volunteer things that they put up with both from other people and themselves. Write these up on the board or flipchart and briefly discuss each one and ask 'What could you do to stop accepting this situation?' Examples are:

What do you put up with from other people?	What do you put up with from yourself?
<ul><li>A colleague who takes advantage of me.</li><li>A friend who I spend time supporting but who never supports me.</li><li>A teenage daughter who never says thank you for anything I do for her.</li><li>Always doing what my sister wants.</li><li>Always being expected to organise things.</li></ul>	<ul><li>Wasting time watching TV programmes that bore me.</li><li>Not making time to visit a sick friend.</li><li>Not redecorating my bedroom.</li><li>Not taking a qualification course to help me get promotion.</li><li>Not saying 'no' to things I don't want to do.</li></ul>

Activity (20 minutes)

Give out Handout 1. Instruct participants to write down five things that they put up with that they would like to change. Once that is complete have each person pair up with someone to discuss ideas about what they could do to stop accepting the situations they have listed. They then complete the form.

Closure (10 minutes)

Have each person in turn, state the first thing that they are going to change, how and when they are going to do it.

Homework (5 minutes)

Each person carries out at least one of their chosen changes. Point out that confidence will grow with each task that is achieved. They will feel their energy begin to grow in a positive way and be more able to do what they want to do. Instruct participants to make notes in their diary about how they feel after they have achieved each goal as they work their way through them. Also point out that when their five goals have been achieved they can sit down and write out another five changes they want to make. This is a process that can be gone through when they feel that energy is being drained away by putting up with things rather then using their energy in a positive way.

Increasing positive energy: Handout 1

Things I put up with I want to change	What I will do to stop accepting the situation:
1	
2	
3	
4	
5	

I will carry this out (deadline) on:

Taking stock of your skills

Aims

- To examine personal skills.
- To discover which skills will help achieve personal goals or dream.
- To plan to develop any additional skills needed to achieve goals or dream.

Preparation

Have available a whiteboard or flipchart and copies of the handouts.

Introduction (10 minutes)

Introduce the aims for the session. Ask each person in turn to state something that they have a talent for and are good at doing. This might be:

- Organising things
- Cooking
- Cleaning
- Writing poems
- Cheering people up
- Mediating between people in conflict
- Charity work

Write the statements on a whiteboard or flipchart.

Activity (25 minutes)

Give out Handout 1. Explain that we all play different roles in our everyday lives. These may include:

- parent
- friend
- handyman
- secretary
- cleaner
- manager
- child minder
- carer
- gardener
- accountant
- peacekeeper
- motivator

Ask participants to get into subgroups of three people. They then discuss and write down the roles they have in life. Each person should be able to come up with at least ten fairly quickly and easily. Now instruct them to choose one role each from their list that they really enjoy and discuss and write down the skills they have developed to fulfil that role. An example might be:

Role	Skills I use to fulfil this role are:
Peacemaker	Listening to and understanding both sides of the conflict. Helping someone see another persons' point of view. Negotiating what is acceptable to both parties. Helping people work out solutions. Giving feedback on behaviour. Good communication skills. Helping people deal with their anger. Supporting people who are stressed.

When the process has been completed ask participants:

- What have they discovered about their range of skills?
- What sort of things might they have skills for that they had not thought about?
- Do the skills fit in with a goal, ambition or dream they have?
- Do they think they would discover many more skills if they carried out this process for all the roles they have in life?

Activity (10 minutes)

Give out Handout 2. Ask each participant to write down a goal, ambition or dream that they have and the skills they have discovered that will help them achieve it. While doing the exercise some group members may have discovered a new direction or ambition that they would like to follow that they had not thought of before. They can write this down as their goal or ambition if they wish and the skills they have discovered to help them achieve it. They will also need to think about any new skills they want to develop and note them down.

Closure (10 minutes)

Group members, in turn, share their goal, ambition or dream, the skills they have discovered they have to help them achieve it and any new skills they may need to develop.

Homework (5 minutes)

Ask group members to repeat the exercise for each of the roles they have written down on Handout 1. As they complete the task for each role they then add any additional skills they have discovered to help them achieve their purpose. When they have completed the ten roles they can continue to write out another ten roles and the skills they have to fulfil these. They then write down their goals and ambitions, the skills they have to achieve them and any new skills they need to develop.

Taking stock of your skills: Handout 1

Roles I have in life are:

1	6
2	7
3	8
4	9
5	10

Role	Skills I use to fulfil this role are:

Taking stock of your skills: Handout 2

My goal, ambition or dream is:

The skills I have to help me achieve this are:

New skills I need to develop are:

The freedom of boundaries

Aims

- To understand what are boundaries.
- To explore personal boundaries.
- To set personal boundaries.

Preparation

Have available a whiteboard or flipchart and copies of the handouts.

Introduction (10 minutes)

Outline the aims for the session. Explain that boundaries are the rules we all set so that other people do not harm us. It is like setting a boundary line around yourself so that other people do not intrude on your space, wellbeing, sensitivities or wishes without being invited to do so. Ask and briefly discuss with the group:

- What are we protecting? (*Right to develop personally, sensitivities, beliefs, feelings, sense of self-worth, harm from physical or verbal abuse, sense of self-respect, right to say 'no' to something not liked, right to equal opportunity and so on.*)
- What happens when we have weak boundaries or none at all? (*Don't get opportunity to develop personally, lack sense of self-worth, become 'needy', open to physical and verbal abuse, lack self-respect, attract disrespectful people who will try to abuse us, fear taking risks, are drained by other people's demands, are subservient, live life through other people – sometimes our own children, always seeking approval from others, worry about others – what they are thinking, lie or withhold the truth to protect self and so on.*)
- What happens when we have strong boundaries? (*Able to develop personally, have a sense of self-respect and worth, have equal opportunity, have more energy, have confidence in self, have respect from others, able to take reasonable risks and so on.*)

Activity (15 minutes)

Give out Handout 1. Using the examples below explain how to use the form. To demonstrate, draw the form on a whiteboard or flipchart and fill in one or two examples.

Person	Unacceptable behaviour	Acceptable behaviour
Manager	Shouting at me in front of others.	Asking to speak to me.
Partner	Belittling my ideas.	Listen to and try to understand my point of view.
Son	Not contributing to household expenses.	Paying an agreed amount each week.

Now ask participants to complete a list, using Handout 1, of unacceptable and acceptable behaviour from other people in their lives. They can do this individually or in pairs, helping each other.

Activity (10 minutes)

Explain to group members that they will need to sit down with the person involved and talk through what they feel is unacceptable behaviour and what they want to happen instead. Instruct participants to work in pairs. Ask them to choose one of the unacceptable behaviours and, having decided what they would like to happen, take turns in role playing the scene, discussing and explaining what they want with the person involved. They do this in turn.

Activity (15 minutes)

State that to ensure that boundaries are maintained it is necessary to be aware of a 'warning trigger' that anticipates that the boundary is close to being challenged. This gives opportunity to remind the other person involved about the boundary. Examples might be:

Person	Boundary	Warning trigger	What I will do
Sister	Belittling my ideas	Not listening	State 'You are not listening, you are watching the TV. Please turn it off and listen to what I am saying.'
Partner	Taking advantage	Saying he has arranged to do something else when he has agreed to look after our daughter	State that he needs to discuss it with me before committing himself to anything else or he will have to cancel it.

Give out Handout 2. Still working in pairs, instruct participant to complete at least one boundary, write down the trigger and what they will do to maintain the boundary and ensure it is not ignored.

Closure (5 minutes)

Each person briefly states a chosen boundary, the warning trigger and what they will do when the boundary is challenged.

Homework (5 minutes)

Instruct individuals to use the process to decide on boundaries they want to set and begin working on them one at a time.

The freedom of boundaries: Handout 1

Person	Unacceptable behaviour	Acceptable behaviour

The freedom of boundaries: Handout 2

Person	Boundary	Warning trigger	What I will do

Learning to Learn

- How I learn
- Overcoming barriers to learning
- Planning to learn
- The learning power of questions

How I learn

Aims

- To understand the best way to learn.
- To identify individual strengths as a learner.
- To explore different ways to learn.

Preparation

Have available a whiteboard or flipchart and copies of the handouts.

Introduction (15 minutes)

Explain the aims for the session. Ask group members and discuss:

- Where does learning take place? (*At home, on courses, at school, work, on holiday, having fun, playing, doing a hobby, watching TV, etc.*)
- At what age does learning take place? (*All ages*)
- Why do we learn something new? (*To get promotion, to get a new job, to make the garden look nice, to impress someone, to have fun, to grow personally, to achieve an ambition, to get more money, to be able to do something well, to cope better with life, etc.*)

Ask for some examples of things people have learned and why they learned it. This might be:

- How to play cricket.
- How to use a computer.
- How to ride a bicycle.
- How to make people laugh.
- How to be assertive.
- How to ask for help.

Write these up on the whiteboard or flipchart. Point out that this means that everyone already has a wide range of learning experience and skills. What they need to do is examine these skills to find out what learning methods work best for them.

Activity (15 minutes)

Give out Handout 1 and ask participants to complete it for up to four good and four bad learning experiences. They will need to think about:

- Both formal and informal learning they have experienced.
- Whether what they were learning interested them.
- How easy or difficult it was.
- What help or support they had.

When the task has been completed ask for volunteers to share some of the things they have found out about how they learn. Ask:

- Did the setting affect them?
- Did the reason they were learning affect the process? In what way?
- Did the degree of difficulty affect them?
- Did any support, or lack of it, affect them?

Activity (15 minutes)

Give out Handout 2 and ask each person to complete the questionnaire. When completed, ask for volunteers to briefly share what they have found out about themselves.

Closure (10 minutes)

Give out Handout 3. When completed, ask each person to briefly state one thing that they can do in the coming week to help their learning.

Homework (5 minutes)

Instruct participants to experiment with their learning style during the coming week adapting how they learn to suit it. Suggest that each time they do this they record any affect it has on their learning and then reflect on affects at the end of the week.

How I learn: Handout 1

Good or successful learning experiences

What I learned	Why I learned this	How I felt

Bad or unsuccessful learning experiences

What I wanted to learn	Why I did not learn	How I felt

What helps me to learn is:

What hinders my learning is:

How I learn: Handout 2

Visual	Yes	No	Auditory	Yes	No	Kinaesthetic	Yes	No
Do you like the use of pictures, diagrams and drawings when being given instructions?			Do you feel most comfortable when given spoken instructions?			Do you like to be shown how to do something?		
Do you use words like 'looks good', 'I see', 'picture this' and 'imagine it'?			Do you use words like 'that sounds good', 'I hear what you're saying' and 'that's in tune'?			Do you use words like 'a light touch', 'it felt good' and 'hold on'?		
Do you prefer face-to-face discussions?			Do you like talking on the phone?			Do you like to talk while doing something?		
Do you like to read newspapers to keep up with the news?			Do you prefer to listen to the radio or TV to keep up with the news?			Do you like role playing and acting things out?		
When you read do you picture the story or what is being described in your mind?			Do you listen to a lot of music in your spare time?			Do you like doing something physically active in your spare time?		
Do you use diagrams and drawings when explaining something?			When planning something do you like to talk it through with someone?			Do you like to demonstrate something when you are explaining it?		
Do you find it easier to remember people's faces than their names?			Do you like discussions and hearing other people's views?			Do you like to feel and touch objects to appreciate them?		

The column in which you have ticked the most 'yes' answers indicates the learning style that suits you best. Most people will use a mixture of styles but may lean towards one or two preferred styles. Knowing your preferred style will assist you to choose the best way for you to learn.

Visual preference learners learn best by:	Auditory preference learners learn best by:	Kinaesthetic preference learners learn best by:
• Seeing. • Using diagrams, maps, posters, displays etc. • Visualising ideas and facts in your mind. • Using planners, organisers and goal setting charts. • Writing things down. • Studying on your own.	• Hearing. • Studying with someone else so you can talk things through. • Repeating things aloud you want to remember. • Making taped notes and playing them aloud. • Listening to lectures. • Having discussions. • Repetition and summary.	• Doing. • Having regular breaks. • Doing something while repeating words aloud. • Practising doing something. • Touching and feeling. • Practical exercises. • Memorise by physically writing information down or in the air.

The above is based on the VAK (Visual, Auditory and Kinaesthetic) learning styles model and is an indicator only of your learning preferences.

How I learn: Handout 3

What motives me to learn is:

My learning style preference is:

Things I can do to help my learning are:

I can use this knowledge in the future to: (make a list of different things you intend doing and state how your new knowledge about your learning can help you)

Overcoming barriers to learning

<hr>

Aims

- To explore barriers to learning.
- To share solutions for overcoming barriers.
- To plan how to overcome personal barriers.

Preparation

Have available a whiteboard or flipchart, copies of the handout, some whiteboard markers and blank pieces of paper and envelopes.

<hr>

Introduction (15 minutes)

Introduce the aims for the session. Explain that barriers are anything that stops or hinders anyone learning something. Examples of barrier statements are:

- I had a bad experience of learning – a teacher humiliated me continuously in front of everyone in the class.
- I have no time to learn.
- My pals have always thought people who learn are snobs and make fun of them.
- I feel too ashamed and embarrassed by my ignorance.
- I can't concentrate for any length of time.
- I'm too old to start learning anything now.
- I'm afraid of failing and looking stupid.

Write a couple of examples on the whiteboard or flipchart. Next, hand everyone a whiteboard marker and invite them all to come out to the front, mill around, and write or draw at least one barrier each on the board. This can be at any angle or place on the board. When this has been completed read though and discuss with the group the effect each barrier has on people and their lives. This might include:

- Unable to get promotion
- Poorer rates of pay
- Unable to fulfil potential
- Less able to help children develop
- Become stressed
- Less able to cope
- Feel inadequate
- Poor self-esteem and confidence

Encourage individuals to speak from experience. Ask how would their lives change if the barriers did not exist?

Activity (30 minutes)

Divide participants into subgroups of three or four people. Give each subgroup a copy of Handout 1. Ask each subgroup to discuss and write down as many of their personal barriers to learning as possible ensuring that everyone has at least one barrier listed.

Allow five minutes or so and then ask each subgroup to give their list of barriers to the subgroup on their right. The subgroups then think of as many alternatives suggestions to overcome the problems on the list they now have as possible. They should have at least two suggestions for each barrier. Examples might be:

Barrier	What I can do to overcome this is:
I'm afraid it might change my relationships.	Talk it over with other people who might be affected, what you fear and how both you and they can deal with it. Talk through with a friend/partner/manager any support you might need to help you cope with any changes.
I have no time to learn.	Find out how much time you will need to learn what you want to learn. Then examine your routine to find out if you can rearrange and stop doing some other things to allow time to learn. Discuss with your partner or boss how you can be supported to enable you to have time to learn.

After about ten minutes, ask each subgroup to present their list of barriers to everyone and their suggested solutions to overcome each one. Allow members of other subgroups to comment and add further suggestions.

Closure (10 minutes)

Ask participants if any of the suggested solutions seem feasible to them. Do they see benefits from identifying barriers, looking at options and getting ideas from others?

Give out some blank pieces of paper and an envelope. Now ask each person to identify a learning task they could undertake during the coming week, write it on the blank sheet of paper and put it in the envelope. This might be to ask their partner or a colleague to show them how to do something, look up in a book how to do something, go to a demonstration, practice doing something, watch an educational programme, etc. It should be a small learning project that is achievable and will enable them to build confidence. Next, they verbally state, in turn, what they are going to do, any perceived barriers, how they will overcome them and when they will carry it out.

Homework (5 minutes)

Briefly discuss any difficulties individuals perceive in the task they have set themselves and have the group offer alternative solutions to the problem. Ask everyone to write their name on the outside of their envelope and hand it to you. Tell them you will open each one at the beginning of the next session to find out how everyone has got on. Finally, instruct everyone to carry out their plan.

Overcoming barriers to learning: Handout 1

Barrier	What I can do to overcome this is:

Planning to learn

Aims

- To explore different methods of learning.
- To decide what to learn.
- To produce a twelve month plan for learning.

Preparation

Have available copies of the handouts and a whiteboard or flipchart.

Introduction (10 minutes)

Explain the aims for the session. Ask participants to call out different ways they have learned something and write the methods up on the whiteboard. This might include:

- Talking to people
- Swapping jobs
- Learning by mistakes
- Using DIY books
- Watching someone else
- Role play
- Using the internet
- Going to a class
- Having a mentor
- Studying
- Problem solving
- Reflecting on experience
- Receiving feedback
- Networking
- Playing games
- Being instructed
- Asking questions
- Trial and error
- Learning by doing
- Sharing knowledge
- Observation visits

Ensure the list of methods of learning is as long as possible. When it has been completed instruct participants to think of which methods that work best for them and then state something they learned using one of the methods. Did they enjoy learning it? Ask group members to also think of some of the methods they have not yet used but might appeal to them.

Activity (20 minutes)

Ask participants if there are things they would like to achieve or do in the next twelve months. After some volunteers have disclosed some of their ambitions give out Handout 1. Have participants work on their own to write down their ambitions and then in pairs to help each other complete what they need to learn to achieve their ambitions. Example ambitions might be:

At work	In my social life	For myself	For my family and friends
Network more. Get promoted to dispatch manager.	Make more friends.	Improve my diet. Learn about local history.	Look after my elderly mother.

What I need to learn to achieve this:

How to do spreadsheets.
Assertiveness skills.
To chair staff meetings.
To cook healthy meals.
Find out about dementia so I can understand what is happening to my mother.

Activity (15 minutes)

Give out Handout 2 and, still working in pairs to help each other, have everyone complete an outline of their plan of learning for the next twelve months. Ensure that participants are aware that they do not need to learn everything they have put on their list. They should choose what will be essential, practical and achievable for them in the time period.

Closure (10 minutes)

Lead a general discussion. Ask:

- How do people feel about their plan?
- Is it realistic and achievable?
- Have they spread the plan over twelve months to make it manageable?
- Does having a plan help them feel in control?
- What are their anxieties and fears?
- What problems and barriers do they see that they will need to overcome? How will they deal these?
- What will be their first step? Do they need to gather in some additional information or talk to other people who might be involved or affected by their plan to enable it to happen?

Homework (5 minutes)

Instruct participants to consult with other people as necessary, obtain further information as required, plan how to deal with any foreseeable problems, then revisit their plan and make any readjustments to make it realistic and achievable.

Planning to learn: Handout 1

What I want to achieve

At work	In my social life	For myself	For my family and friends

What I need to learn to achieve this is:

Planning to learn: Handout 2

My learning plan

What I am going to learn is:	My reason for learning it is:	My preferred methods to learn it are:	When I will learn it:	Where I am going to learn it:

The learning power of questions

Aims

- To understand the importance of asking questions with an aim.
- To encourage participants to think about and plan questions.
- To apply questions and research to everyday living and situations.

Preparation

Have available copies of the handouts.

Introduction (5 minutes)

Introduce the aims for the session. Explain that asking good questions helps us explore what we want to learn, expand our knowledge and obtain information to achieve what we want. To be able to ask good questions we need to be creative in how we think, to ensure we get the answer that best suits our needs. Sometimes we need to work backwards. This entails thinking about the information we want to obtain and then posing a question that extracts it.

Activity (15 minutes)

Give out Handout 1 and ask participants to work in pairs to think up the questions that resulted in the answers provided. When completed, have group members share and discuss the questions they have created. Ask:

- How difficult was it to find a question that provided the answer?
- What was the aim of the person asking the question?
- Did the question provide a useful answer?
- How can we tell if a question is useful?
- Why is asking the correct questions important?
- In what situations is it important to ask questions?
- How does asking questions help us learn?

Activity (10 minutes)

Give out Handout 2 and go through the step-by-step process outlined.

Step 1: What I am researching is: (*Should I rent my spare room out to a student?*)

Because: (*I want extra money to help me pay the mortgage*)

Step 2: Questions I need answered are: (*What sort of lodger do I want? What ground rules will I need to agree? How much would a lodger pay? Should I get references? Where would I advertise? etc.*)

Step 3: I am going to get the answers to my questions by: (*Checking what other people are charging for a similar room. Asking for advice from someone I know who rents out a room. Finding out advertising rates in the local paper etc.*)

Step 4: What have I found out is: (*List the answers to the questions*)

Step 5: My conclusion is: (*Having obtained answers to all the questions make a decision or draw a conclusion from the evidence gathered*)

Activity (15 minutes)

Split the participants into small sub-groups and give each sub-group a topic to research, investigate or a mystery to solve. Instruct them to complete steps 1 to 4 in order for them to successfully complete the task or solve the mystery. Use the examples in Handout 3 or create topics more suited to your particular group. Alternatively, if appropriate and participants are confident, ask group members to complete the steps for something a group member needs to research or learn.

Closure (10 minutes)

Have the sub-groups feed back their completed steps. In each case explore if the questions asked and the actions to obtain the answers are appropriate to obtain the information needed to achieve the initial goal (Step 1).

Homework (5 minutes)

Instruct participants to apply the method to researching something they want to learn or find out about during the coming week. This might be to do a course of learning, where to go on holiday, whether to share a flat with someone, how to do something and so on. Remind them that once they have the answers to their questions they then need to list the answers and use the information to draw a conclusion.

The learning power of questions: Handout 1

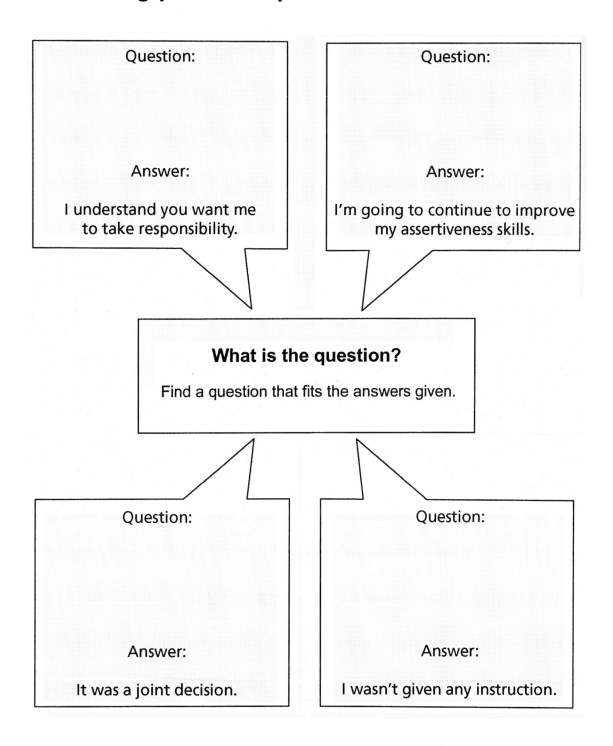

The learning power of questions: Handout 2

Step 1: What I am researching is:

Because:

Step 2: Questions I need answered are:

Step 3: I am going to get the answers to my questions by: (Plan of action)

Step 4: What I have found out is:

Step 5: My conclusion is:

The learning power of questions: Handout 3

Topic 1

John works as a van driver delivering engineering components. He has decided he wants to change his job. He feels there is no opportunity for him to advance his career with his current company and that extra time he puts in to deliver parts in emergencies is not appreciated. It is taken for granted. It also means he spends a lot of time away overnight from his family and has less time to support his wife and child. He has seen a similar job advertised with a company that promises advancement opportunities but does not state what the opportunities are.

Topic 2

A group of young people have gone swimming together in the local swimming pool. When they return to get dressed one of them finds that their wallet and watch have gone missing. You are the assistant manager of the pool and have been told to investigate. What questions would you want answered to find out what has happened to the wallet and watch?

Topic 3

You are going travelling in a tropical country. In the area you will be passing though there may be danger from groups rioting, disease and ferocious animals. What questions would you want answered to ensure you have a safe visit?

Topic 4

You are setting up business as a window cleaner and have limited money. You want to purchase a vehicle that you can use both for work and leisure. What questions would you want answered before making a purchase?

© Robin Dynes. *Instant Session Plans for Essential Life Skills: Learning and Development.* www.russellhouse.co.uk

Becoming Self-motivated

- What motivates me?
- Creating a vision
- Active motivating strategies
- Watch your language!

What motivates me?

Aims

- To understand personal motivation.
- To recognise the benefits of sharing this information.
- To use the knowledge to aid learning.

Preparation

Have available copies of the handouts, a whiteboard or flipchart and a soft ball or object.

Introduction (5 minutes)

Discuss the aims for the session and what is meant by personal or self-motivation. Ask the group to come up with a definition of what motivation is and write it on the board. A definition might be:

It is the skill of inspiring and activating yourself to do or achieve something positive.

When you are sure the concept has been understood by everyone ask:

Why should we bother to understand what motivates us?

Again, write the suggestions up on a whiteboard of flipchart. Typical answers might include:

- Increases my enthusiasm to do something.
- Helps stimulate my interest.
- Being highly motivated would help me keep going when I encounter difficulties.
- Being motivated would help me focus and concentrate.
- Good motivation improves chances of succeeding.
- Makes it enjoyable and fun to do something.

Activity (10 minutes)

Now draw a circle on the board and write 'motivators' in it as shown in Handout 1. Have the group members call out the things which motivate them and people in general. Write these on the board or flipchart to form a spider type drawing as in the handout. When plenty of legs have been added to the spider give out copies of Handout 1.

Activity (10 minutes)

Give out copies of Handout 2 and instruct participants to draw in their own personal motivators – the things that in their experience motivate them to do things.

Activity (20 minutes)

Form three subgroups. Give out Handout 3 and ask each subgroup to discuss and write down on the handout:

1. What they think might be gained from sharing their motivators with other people (*Obtain their support, get feedback on progress from them, obtain guidance, etc.*)
2. With whom it might be appropriate to share their motivators. Would they share all of them with everyone? (*Line manager for work project, carer or parent for independence, etc.*)
3. How might this then be used to aid their learning and achievement? (*Line manager give feedback on progress, carer give advice and guidance, etc.*)

When completed have:

- Subgroup 1 share with the whole group what they have concluded about what is to be gained.
- Subgroup 2 state with whom it may be appropriate to share this information.
- Subgroup 3 state how the information can be used to motivate their learning and achievements.

As each subgroup gives their feedback encourage members of the other subgroups to comment and add to the feedback.

Closure (10 minutes)

Write the following up on the board:

- *'Something I have to learn or do in the coming week is . . .'*
- *'What motivates me to do it is . . .'*
- *'The person it would be appropriate to share this with is . . .'*
- *'How this will help/encourage me to do it is . . .'*

Allow a moment or two for thought and then throw a soft ball or object to one of the participants and ask them to make their statement. This person then throws the soft ball or object to another participant and they make their statement until everyone has had a go. Encourage group members to help each other when they are struggling with their statements.

Homework (5 minutes)

Instruct participants to carry out their chosen learning or task, then record and reflect how it felt and whether understanding their motivation and using it to boost their incentive helped.

What motivates me? Handout 1

What motivates me? Handout 2

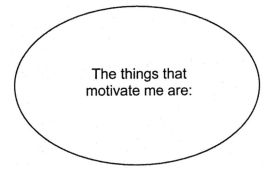

The things that
motivate me are:

What motivates me? Handout 3

What is to be gained by sharing our personal motivators with other people?

Who would share you share your motivators with? Would you share all of them with everyone?

How can sharing this information be used to aid your learning and ability to achieve?

Creating a vision

Aims

- To understand the importance of having a vision.
- To examine the effect of creating a vision.
- To create a personal vision.

Preparation

Have copies of the handouts available, colouring pencils etc. with which to draw.

Introduction (5 minutes)

Go through the aims for the session. Explain that having a vision entails having imaginative insight into the future about how we want it to be. This vision provides us with the drive and motivation to make that vision come true. Ask if anyone in the group has experienced really wanting to achieve, obtain or do something. This might have been a dress they wanted, a boyfriend they wanted to date or a place they wanted to visit. What effect did this have on how they went about achieving and doing it? Did it make them determined? Did they go to great lengths and overcome some difficulties to do it? That is having a vision.

Activity (10 minutes)

Give out Handout 1. Go through the process outlined and discuss the example given. Explain how, once we have created, a vision we can build on it to keep the energy and motivation going until we have achieved our goal.

Activity (15 minutes)

Give out Handout 2. Ask participants to choose one of the following: work, leisure, relationships or family. Instruct them to sit back, close their eyes and imagine something they really want in one of these areas. This might be to get a qualification, improve a specific relationship in some way, have a family holiday, how they want that part of their life to be in one years' time and so on. Now ask them to imagine that this has happened. What do they see, hear, smell, taste and feel? What difference has it made? What changes have occurred? Tell them to hold this vision for a moment and savour it in every detail.

Now instruct them to write about their vision or draw it on the handout or a combination of both. Encourage them to use as much detail as possible. On the bottom they sum up their vision in one sentence, keeping it specific.

Activity (15 minutes)

Now have participants pair up with someone to discuss and suggest what additional motivators can used to reinforce each others visions. They write these down on Handout 2.

Closure (10 minutes)

Ask the participants how they now feel about their vision. Is it something they now feel confident enough about to plan and take action to make it come true? Invite volunteers to share their vision and motivators with the whole group.

Homework (5 minutes)

Instruct everyone to plan to make their vision come true and take the first steps towards their goal. Explain that it is good to use the process for a long-term vision such as what they would like their lives to be like in five years time. How would they want their relationships, work, leisure and family life to be? The process can then provide them with the motivation to achieve what they want in life. Invite them to spend time during the coming week creating their vision for their future. Area headings can be changed to suit different circumstances.

Creating a vision: Handout 1

My vision
A strong vision energises, stimulates, motivates and impels you forward. The vision must be specific and compelling.

Example

My vision
Passing my driving test by the end of August.

Confidence to take action
A vision that you believe in helps to build confidence to plan and take action. Add other motivators such as 'Doing this will earn me the respect of my colleagues', 'This will help me ensure a better future for my family', and so on.

Confidence to take action
I can do this in four months. It will impress my girlfriend and my mates. When I pass, I can apply for one of the sales jobs – that means status and more money.

Taking action
Work out a simple plan, recruit help and support. Incorporate rewards and celebrations into your plans as you move forward. Keep revisiting and reinforcing your initial vision.

Taking action
If I work on Saturday morning I can afford to take a driving lesson most weeks. Mum will help me learn the highway code and I can ask Uncle Jason to take me out to practice driving every Sunday. I will take Mum out for a meal to celebrate when I pass the highway code test. And, at the end of each month, I will go bowling with Uncle Jason to celebrate my progress and thank him.

Review and obtain feedback
Map and acknowledge your progress towards the vision. Reinforce this with other people's perception of your success – no matter how small each step. See obstacles as problems to be solved and part of the learning process.

Review and obtain feedback
My driving instructor, Jason and Mum will tell me how I'm doing and encourage me. They will also help me overcome any difficulties. I will keep a diary of my progress.

Responding to feedback
Be flexible. If you do not see an immediate solution move on to something else that builds towards the vision. Be willing to change your approach and adjust plans. Learn from experience. Ask 'How could I have done this differently?' Praise yourself for learning from your mistakes as well as successes.

Responding to feedback
Uncle Jason says I need to practice three point turns, parking and reversing. I failed my theory test first go. I need to think ahead about road hazards and be able to recognise them. I can get a video to practice identifying them. I know what I did wrong so I can make sure I get it right next time. I have made a few misjudgements but I am learning from them.

Creating a vision: Handout 2

Choose one of the following topics: **work**, **leisure**, **relationships** or **family**. Close your eyes and imagine what you really want in your chosen area. Imagine it has happened in as much detail as possible. See it, feel it, smell it, taste it and hear it. Now draw it in the space below, write about it or use a combination of both in as much detail as possible.

My vision

My additional motivators are

Active motivating strategies

Aims

- To explore a range of strategies to motivate.
- To discover which motivators work best for individuals.
- To learn to use different motivators.

Preparation

Have available copies of the handout and a whiteboard or flipchart.

Introduction (15 minutes)

Explain the aims for the session. Ask participants to line up in a row with the tallest on the left and the shortest on the right. Now give each person a number starting with one. Next instruct the odd numbered individuals to pair up with someone who has been given an even number. Partners now discuss and share a special or unusual skill, talent or ability they have. This may be an ability to make friends, write stories, draw cartoons, do funny walks, play marbles, recite poetry, imitate famous people or colleagues, sing in the shower, cook unusual meals or make funny noises and so on. The more odd or peculiar the talent is the better. After a few minutes stop the proceedings and ask participants to state their partner's name and their special talent. Invite a few demonstrations if possible. Humour should emerge during these proceedings. Ask how they feel and if providing a bit of fun has made them feel easier, more confident and motivated to face the rest of the session.

Activity (25 minutes)

Give out Handout 1. Go through and discuss the strategies listed. Ask if participants have tried any of them. Did it work? Why did it work? If it did not work, was there a reason? Remind people that each person is an individual and that each strategy will not work for everyone – nor in all circumstances. Has anyone used other strategies? Write these up on the whiteboard or flipchart.

Instruct each person to go through the list and tick the methods they think might work for them. From the whiteboard they can add any suggestions to their personal list that they feel would be useful.

Closure (15 minutes)

Ask each person to think about the strategies they have ticked and choose one or two that they would like to experiment with and how and when they will use them during the coming week. Each person, in turn, then states their chosen strategy or strategies and how they are going to use them.

Homework (5 minutes)

Instruct each person to carry out their intention. Provide opportunity for discussion of any fears or envisaged difficulties.

Active motivating strategies: Handout 1

The journey to the achievement of our vision is beset with detours, flat tyres, breakdowns, obstructions, tedium and diversions. Sometimes it is smooth and everything goes well, at other times life intervenes with diversions such as divorce, financial difficulties, a family member becomes ill and accidents. Here are some strategies for you to consider which will help keep you motivated to achieve your vision.

- Reward yourself for each successful step – no matter how small.
- Begin by setting small goals. Having goals that are fairly easy to achieve makes it easier to make a start. Once a first step has been taken, no matter how small, you will have more motivation for the rest of the journey.
- Create a symbol for yourself to remind you of your strengths and goals when your resolve begins to weaken. For example: imagine yourself as a solid oak tree when your confidence feels weak.
- Avoid people who are negative. They tend to erode resolve.
- Regularly remind yourself of past successes.
- Treat mistakes as opportunities to learn.
- Plan for difficulties and setbacks.
- Nurture supportive relationships. Make friends with people who are positive and supportive.
- Define yourself by something you feel good about: 'I am a good parent', 'I am a good friend', 'I am a good worker' and so on.
- Remind yourself that you do not have to be perfect and neither does your work.
- Strengthen your reasons for attaining your goals by choosing reasons that are true to you: 'I want to grow as a person', 'I want to earn more money' and so on. Constantly remind yourself of these reasons.
- Keep a scrap book about activities you have enjoyed or feel proud about.
- Share your goals with people who will encourage you.
- Praise yourself regularly: 'That was difficult, but I managed to do it.', 'I made a good job of that.'
- Have quiet moments when you imagine what success will feel like. Visualise it using all the senses.
- Have a clear vision of how you want things to be in the future.
- Be prepared to move out of your comfort zone and take some risks.
- Turn negative thoughts into positive ones: 'I am stupid' becomes 'I can use the knowledge I have gained from this to do it better next time'
- Use humour. Laugh at yourself and your own idiosyncrasy.
- When you do not feel like doing something or feel yourself drifting from your goal take a few minutes to refocus. Coach yourself by saying things like: 'I am going to put my goals first. I am going to spend the next fifteen minutes exercising. I will lose ten pounds by August. It is more important than watching TV'.
- Set realistic targets. Review and break down unrealistic targets into smaller, achievable steps.
- Ask for help when you need it.

- Recognise and acknowledge your skills.
- Have regular meetings with like minded people for mutual support.
- Keep a 'positive journal'.
- Search out a mentor or coach with whom you can explore ideas and who will give you guidance.
- Know what motivates you and use this knowledge.
- Know and use your preferred learning styles to advantage.

Watch your language!

Aims

- To explore the use of metaphors in how we think and see the world.
- To learn how to create metaphors that motivate.
- To use language that motivates.

Preparation

Have available copies of the handouts and a whiteboard or flipchart.

Introduction (10 minutes)

Discuss the aims for the session. Explain that how we use words to express ourselves influences how we see the world. If we continually use negative words and expressions we become predisposed to a negative view of the world. This:

- Takes away the motivation to do things.
- Puts up barriers that seem impossible to overcome.
- Blocks our thinking and ability to progress.

Ask the participants:

What do you think and say when you are feeling at your lowest? (Write the answers on a whiteboard of flipchart) Answers will likely include words and expressions like:

'I have no energy'.	'I'm a failure'.
'I can't do anything'.	'Life is hell'.
'I'm hopeless'.	'I could never do that.'

Now ask participants:

What do you think and say when you are feeling at your best? (Again, write the answers on a whiteboard or flipchart.) Answers will likely include words and expressions like:

'I can get on with things'.	'Life is exciting'.
'I'm full of energy'.	'The world is my oyster'.
'I can do this'.	'I can risk trying this'.

Point out that often the negative expressions take over and predominate. However, if we become aware of how we use words and express ourselves we can change these to motivate and trigger the way we feel when at our best.

Activity (20 minutes)

Explain that a metaphor is an unusual way of saying something in which one thing is compared with another. It is a comparison between two objects not usually thought to have anything in common. A great fighter is said to be 'a lion in battle'. Other examples are: 'the kettle sings', 'I've hit a brick wall', 'life is a lottery', 'life is a constant storm', 'life is a roller coaster adventure', 'life is a box of Turkish delight', etc. It does not mean it in a literal sense.

When the concept of a metaphor has been understood give out Handout 1. Instruct each individual to write in the squares how they would describe a garden, a journey and a house that represents their life. They can write down anything that comes to mind or draw it. They then write a metaphor for how they see their life now. They can use something from one of the descriptions they have written or drawn. Alternatively, they can think of something else that they feel represents their life better.

When completed, give out Handout 2 and instruct them to repeat the process to create a metaphor for how they would like their life to be.

Activity (15 minutes)

Ask the group members if they have noticed the type of words and phrases they use on a regular basis. Is there a bias towards using negative language? Some examples are given in Handout 3. Invite volunteers to call out a few examples of words and phrases they use on a regular basis which might indicate a negative attitude. Rephrase and restate them on the whiteboard or flipchart using more positive language as shown in the handout examples.

Now give out Handout 3 and instruct participants to think of negative words and phrases they use, write them down and think of a different, more positive way they could make the statement. Some people will find thinking up the positive statement really hard to do. They may need some suggestions.

Closure (10 minutes)

Have participants choose a partner. Partners briefly discuss one thing each person could do during the coming week to work towards making their metaphor come true. Participants then state their partners' metaphor to the whole group and the thing they can do during the coming week to work towards making it come true.

Homework (5 minutes)

Instruct participants to keep their metaphor representing the life they want in mind and carry out the thing they can do to start making it come true. They should display their metaphor in a place where they can see it as often as possible each day. Also, tell them to be conscious of their language and make a note of any negative words and phrases they are using. They then, in a convenient moment, think of a more positive way to rephrase them and consciously replace the negative language each time it comes to mind.

Watch your language! Handout 1

My life now

If my life was a garden the sort of garden
it would be is . . .

If my life was a journey the sort of journey
it would be is . . .

If my life was a house the sort of house
it would be is . . .

Now write a metaphor for how your life is now.

My life is . . .

Watch your language! Handout 2

How I would like life to be

If my life was a garden the sort of garden
it would be is . . .

If my life was a journey the sort of journey
it would be is . . .

If my life was a house the sort of house
it would be is . . .

Now write a metaphor for how you would like your life to be.

My life would be . . .

Watch your language! Handout 3

Negative language	Positive language
'Too big a barrier.'	'The way round this is . . .'
'I have no chance.'	'I could improve my chances by . . .'
'I have no time to do this.'	'If someone covered for me I could . . .'
'I get confused.'	'If I focus on one thing at a time I can do this.'

Self-coaching

- To be a life coach
- Changing your attitude
- Monitoring progress and avoiding inertia
- When the going gets tough

To be a life coach

Aims

- To gain an understanding of what a coach does.
- To decide what you want to coach yourself to do or be.
- To discover some coaching techniques.

Preparation

Have available photocopies of the handouts, a whiteboard or flipchart and some mirrors.

Introduction (10 minutes)

Outline the aims for the session. Ask: *'What comes to mind when you think of a coach?'* Ideas will likely include:
– Football coach
– Fitness coach
– Dance coach
– Swimming coach
Now ask: *'If you had a coach what would you expect him to do?'* Write the suggestions up on the whiteboard. This may include:

- Support me.
- Help get the best from me.
- Give me feedback on how I'm doing.
- Assess what point I'm at and how far I have to go.
- Help me set goals.
- Point out my strengths.
- Point out areas I need to strengthen.
- Tell me where to focus my efforts.

Activity (15 minutes)

Next ask and briefly discuss: *'Have you ever had anyone coach you or encourage you to do something?'* Who was it – a parent, a friend, a teacher, a colleague?

Give out Handout 1. Discuss the examples given and then instruct everyone to write down who has coached them, what that person did to encourage them and what they could do to coach themselves.

End the activity by getting everyone to share some of the ways they have decided they could coach themselves.

Activity (5 minutes)

Give out some hand mirrors – one for each person. These can be small mirrors. Now invite them to look in the mirrors and meet their new coach. Invite them to say to their reflection in the mirror: *'You are my brand new personal coach. What you are going to do is . . .'* They repeat some of the ways that they have decided they can coach and encourage themselves. They may feel self-conscious doing this but emphasise it is something they can do in the mirror at home.

Activity (15 minutes)

State that coaches coach individuals to do something so the first step is to decide what they want to do. Give out Handout 2. Ask participants to write down up to ten things they want to do. This might be things like:

- Get a better job.
- Improve a relationship.
- Keep fit and healthy.
- Save for a holiday.
- Set boundaries with your children.
- Pass an exam.

Having made a list, individuals decide which goal is most important for them and they want to give priority to.

Explain that in order to know what progress they are making they need to have a base line or starting point. They can do this by writing their priority goal in the 'How I feel now' chart and marking the level they feel they are at now. For example, if my priority goal was to improve a relationship I feel is poor I might mark my current position as a 2. They also write the date.

Having a starting point, they now decide how often they are going to measure their progress. This will depend on the goal and the time limit they set themselves to achieve it. For example, when working to improve my relationship I may set a month to achieve my goal and decide to measure my progress once or twice a week. If on the other hand, I knew reaching my goal would likely take about a year I might decide to measure my progress once or twice a month. It is probably better to err on the side of measuring progress more often than having long time gaps. This enables you to see the pattern emerging more clearly.

Do point out that in working towards a goal there will be ups and downs. If the pattern emerging shows that little or no progress is being made or the situation is becoming worse because of any action taken, the person needs to review the situation and set specific tasks to get back on track. Also, warn that seeing constant progress can sometimes lead to complacency. Work will still need to be done on skills or actions.

Closure (10 minutes)

Write up on the whiteboard or flipchart:

My priority goal is . . .

I will coach myself by . . .

I will measure my progress . . .

Each participant, in turn, then makes statements using these sentence beginnings.

Homework (5 minutes)

Instruct participants to start coaching themselves towards their chosen goal.

To be a life coach: Handout 1

People who have coached and encouraged me	What they did
My mother	She listened. She asked questions to help me examine the problem. She made suggestions. She told me what was good. She told me I had the ability to succeed.
My manager Raj	He helped me set challenging but achievable targets. He encouraged me to think about my future and the different routes I could take. He congratulated me when I achieved set goals. He challenged some of my negative thinking.

Things I could do to encourage and coach myself are:

1.   4.

2.   5.

3.   6.

To be a life coach: Handout 2

Ten things I want to do

1.

2.

3.

4.

5.

6.

7.

8.

9.

10.

How I feel now chart

My priority goal is:	Poor									Good	Date
	1	2	3	4	5	6	7	8	9	10	
	1	2	3	4	5	6	7	8	9	10	
	1	2	3	4	5	6	7	8	9	10	
	1	2	3	4	5	6	7	8	9	10	
	1	2	3	4	5	6	7	8	9	10	

Changing your attitude

Aims

- To learn to challenge personal attitudes.
- To practice a process to change personal attitudes.
- To relate the process to personal situations.

Preparation

Have available a whiteboard or flipchart and photocopies of the handout.

Introduction (15 minutes)

Discuss the aims for the session. State that often we make excuses for not taking an opportunity, doing or achieving something. We look for excuses not to do it and state them as reasons. Coaching yourself entails challenging these excuses and not opting out.

Ask participants to think of something they have really wanted to do or achieve now or in the recent past and have dismissed or shelved it. Invite volunteers to share a couple of these and write them up on the board. Next, ask them what they told themselves about doing these things that resulted in them not doing or putting off doing them. Also write these up on the board. The result should look something like:

What I wanted to do	What I told myself
Apply for a promotion.	I haven't got the skills. I'm not good enough. Sue will apply, she's better than me. I'll look stupid if I fail. My experience is limited.
Save money for a holiday.	My husband spends all the extra money on the kids. The children will blame me if they can't have what they want. My husband will sulk. I'll get angry and take it out on everyone. It's too much hassle.

Now ask:

- When you have given yourself these excuses what happens to your attitude towards achieving your goal?
- Do you abandon doing anything about it?
- How do you then feel?
- Would you like to change this?

Activity (15 minutes)

Take one of the examples given in the previous activity and write the goal across the top of the board or flipchart as in the example in Handout 1. Write down all the excuses for not taking up the opportunity or doing what was intended. Next, working together as a group, complete the 'Reason for doing it' column and the 'Actions I can take' section.

When the example has been examined and understood ask the group members if they can see how the excuses for not doing something can be converted into reasons for doing it with benefits. Also, give out Handout 1 for them to keep as an example.

Activity (15 minutes)

Give out Handout 2. Ask participants to have a go at thinking of something they want or have wanted to do or an opportunity they want to take, but have been making excuses to themselves not to do it. They then use the process to change their attitude towards it.

Closure (10 minutes)

Discuss:

- Did the process help them think through the issues involved?
- What was difficult? What was easy?
- Does the process give back control of the situation?
- How do they feel about their goal now?
- Has their attitude towards it changed?

Where individuals have had difficulty thinking through the reasons for achieving their goal or actions to take have the group discuss and make suggestions to help them complete the process.

Homework (5 minutes)

Instruct participants to carry out their intentions for the goal set in the exercise or apply the process to another goal that they have a poor attitude towards achieving.

Suggest that they keep a journal of their attitude before carrying out the process, what they felt when they had completed thinking it through and while and after carrying out the actions.

Changing your attitude: Handout 1

Goal: To save money for a holiday

Excuses for not doing this are:	Reasons for doing it are:
• My husband spends all our extra money on the children.	• This is not good for the children. They are not learning they can't have everything they want. They need to learn that to gain something they sometimes have to make compromises.
• The children will blame me for stopping them getting what they want.	• They need to learn to respect boundaries and our decisions as parents.
• My husband will sulk if I lay down the rules.	• He needs to accept joint responsibility for setting boundaries and not opt out.
• I will get upset and angry and take it out on everyone.	• If I don't address this now it is just going to get worse. My relationships with my husband and the children will suffer.
• It's too much hassle.	• Everyone has said they want a holiday. We will all be disappointed and upset if we don't have one.

Actions I can take are:

• Talk the issues through with my husband and decide how we are going to set boundaries so we act in the same way, avoid blaming each other, him sulking and me getting upset and angry.

• Together discuss and agree with the children that they do want a holiday and that this means curbing other spending.

Changing your attitude: Handout 2

Goal: _____

Excuses for not doing this are:	Reasons for doing it are:

Actions I can take are:

Monitoring progress and avoiding inertia

Aims

- To give yourself pep talks to avoid inertia.
- To monitor progress using a journal.
- To gain insight from your journal.

Preparation

Have available a whiteboard or flipchart and copies of the handouts.

Introduction (15 minutes)

Go through the aims for the session. Point out that a pep talk is intended to make someone feel more courageous and enthusiastic. It is:

- A spirited, and often, emotional, confrontation.
- An attention getting jolt to energise and mobilise a person into action.

In a pep talk someone gets tough with you. There is no room for 'if', 'but', can't' or 'won't'. Your coach needs to be completely positive and encouraging – there is no room for doubt or hesitation.

There are times when we all want to resist change and doubts crowd in. Our inner coach then needs to tell us to get on with it ('kick butt').

Ask participants to think of something they needed to do in the past or need to do now but feel 'apathetic' and a sense of 'inertia' towards it. Now suggest they think of someone they think of as inspirational from the past or present. This might be a teacher, a well-known football coach, a historic or fictional character or a well-known personality, like Muhammad Ali. Each person now thinks what that person would say to them to jolt them out of their inertia and into action. Instruct everyone to write down the statements on a sheet of paper.

After a few moments ask for volunteers to share what the task was they felt inertia towards and what their coach said to them. Participants then keep these statements to use when they feel apathy settling in towards doing something.

Activity (30 minutes)

State that a good way of monitoring your progress and coaching yourself while learning from experience is to keep a journal. An exercise book, a page a day diary or Handouts 3 and 4 that you will give them can be used to do this. (Handout 4 would need to be photocopied; the pages dated and kept in a folder of some sort.)

Step 1: Writing down their vision and goals to be monitored

Give out Handout 1. Go through it with the group and discuss each section with the participants.

State that each person needs to be clear about their vision for the next year or a set period. A good way to do this is for them to imagine themselves in a years' time. How do they want a particular area of life to be?

The example shows someone's vision in four areas of his life, work, leisure, family and personal. Explain that participants might just want to work on one area or different areas such as health, relationships, education, social life, etc. They can change the headings or have one or two headings to suit their lives and priorities.

From their vision they set their goals.

Next they write their motivation or reason they want to achieve these goals.

Finally, they write down the values that are important to them. Values may include honesty, success, freedom, kindness, independence, trust, power, acceptance, excitement, adventure, children, humour, success, understanding etc.

Values are very important. When they have written down the values they need to check that their vision, goals and motivation do not conflict with their values. For example, if a person's value is that family loyalty is important then the person's vision and goals should agree and not oppose or conflict with that belief. If it does then this will be a de-motivating factor and present problems in achieving the goal.

Point out that although this sounds like a lot to do, it only has to be done once a year, though they might want to review it every three or four months to ensure their vision and goals have not changed in any way. It will also be a good motivator to remind them where they are going and to help them keep focused.

If not too much time has been taken up with discussion or you can extend the session time, it is helpful at this stage to complete an example on the whiteboard working as a group using a vision for the year suggested by one of the participants. Keep it simple, use only one suggested area such as work or leisure and one goal.

Step 2: Writing the journal

Give out Handout 2. Explain that using their goals as a guide they write down what they plan to do during the week which will contribute to achieving their goals.

Then each day during the week they record what happens as they carry out their actions. This should include:

- Traps fallen into, such as negative self-talk.
- Good things that happen.
- Insights into their behaviour and reactions.
- Feedback from other people.
- Any incidents or problems and their reactions.

- Use of motivating tactics such as 'kicking butt'.
- How they are feeling.

Doing this will only take a few minutes towards the end of each day.

Step 3: Reflecting on the week, what has been achieved and learned

At the end of the week the person reads through and reflects on the week, writes down what has been achieved, what has been learned and what actions need to be carried forward to the following week as in the example. From this they can then decide what to include in their plan of action for the following week. They should also remember to celebrate, reward and congratulate themselves in some way for any achievements.

Emphasise that once the procedure is set up it only takes a few minutes each day and around fifteen minutes or so at the end of the week. Once the habit has been formed they will do it automatically.

Closure (10 minutes)

Ask participants to work with the person on their left hand side. Partners now discuss and suggest to each other what they can use for themselves to 'kick butt'. They might like to think back to the person they thought of in the introduction activity and what that person might say to them. Examples might be: 'Don't argue. Just do it!', 'Get out there and slay them', 'Stop thinking, go for it!', 'Get off your bottom and get on with it', etc. Participants then share the slogan their partner is going to use to 'kick butt'.

Homework (5 minutes)

Participants practice 'kicking butt' when they feel inertia and start the journal they are going to use to coach themselves and monitor their progress.

Monitoring progress and avoiding inertia: Handout 1

My vision for the next year is:

Work	Leisure	Family	Personal
Being promoted.	Being able to swim. Producing a short book of poems.	Making an easier life for Dad.	Having a better relationship with my girlfriend. Being a committee member at the youth club.

My goals for the next 12 months are:

Work	To study for a qualification so I get a promotion.
Leisure	To learn to swim. To write and put together a short book of poems.
Family	To help Dad around the house.
Personal	To share my feelings, problems and plans with my girlfriend. To work as a volunteer at the youth club and run for the committee.

My motivation is:

Work	To gain status, respect, money and security.
Leisure	To have fun, have time for myself, impress my girlfriend.
Family	To make Dad feel appreciated for all the help and support he has given me and sacrifices he has made since Mum died.
Personal	To build a closure relationship with my girlfriend and show her I trust her. To contribute to the local community – they supported us when my Mum died. Show my girlfriend I can act responsibly and don't always act the fool.

My values are: (things that are important to me)

- Loyalty to my family and community.
- Being well thought of and respected.
- Having security.
- Feeling loved and having close relationships.
- Having fun and being creative.

Monitoring progress and avoiding inertia: Handout 2

What I plan to do this week:
- *Discuss my plan for getting promotion with my girlfriend and ask her how she feels about it.*
- *Cut the hedges and clear up the garden for Dad.*
- *Get some information about a suitable course I can do.*
- *Go for a swimming lesson.*
- *Spend an hour doing my poetry.*

Sunday

Cut the hedges and cleared the garden. Felt really good. Dad was pleased and told me I did a really good job and he appreciated my effort. Said he was proud of me.

Monday

Discussed my plans for getting promotion with my girlfriend. She was pleased and thought it was a good idea.

Tuesday

Went to the swimming pool after work. Didn't go well. My instructor got angry because I didn't listen to him. I mucked about, bumped into and splashed other people. They didn't like it. I found it difficult. I was scared of sinking and looking stupid in front of the others and started messing about to cover up.

Wednesday

Was going to tell my boss about wanting to do a course but didn't. Stopped myself at the last minute. It's a big commitment. I'll have to do it if I mention it. Felt nervous and frightened.

Thursday

Didn't spend time doing my poetry. Kept thinking what some of the other lads said when they found out I was writing poetry. 'Girls and wimpy swots write poetry', 'Who's a big soft girl, then.' Need to challenge these thoughts. Lots of men write poetry.

Friday

Got information about the course I need to do – it looks daunting. What if I tell my boss I am going to do it and then I'm not good enough? I will look stupid. My girlfriend will think I'm stupid and a wimp too. I need to challenge these thoughts. A more helpful thought would be 'I will earn their respect by having a go'.

Saturday

Talked to Dad. He agreed I would earn respect by having a go and told me to stop thinking about it and get signed up for the course. Also advised me to tell my girlfriend how I felt. He said she would understand my fears and encourage me.

What I have achieved this week:

- *Cut the hedges and cleared the garden.*
- *Discussed my plans with my girlfriend.*
- *Got information about the course I want to do.*
- *Went swimming.*

What I have learned:

- *I am very concerned about looking silly or stupid in front of other people and of failing to achieve.*
- *I mess about to cover up.*
- *I need to challenge my thinking and 'kick butt' as far as my poetry and joining the course is concerned.*
- *I need to discuss my fears with my girlfriend. It will also help me build my relationship with her and show I trust her.*

What I need to carry forward:

- *Signing up for the class (once committed I will feel I have to make the effort to succeed).*
- *Making a commitment to my boss (will help my motivation once committed).*
- *Challenging my negative thoughts and replacing them with more positive thoughts.*
- *Stop messing about to cover up my fears. It is not the end of the world if I look silly. I can learn from my mistakes.*

Monitoring progress and avoiding inertia: Handout 3

My vision for next year is:

Work	Leisure	Family	Personal

My goals for the next 12 months are:

Work	
Leisure	
Family	
Personal	

My motivation is:

Work	
Leisure	
Family	
Personal	

My values are: (things that are important to me)

-
-
-
-
-
-
-

Monitoring progress and avoiding inertia: Handout 4

What I plan to do this week:

Sunday

Monday

Tuesday

Wednesday

Thursday

Friday

Saturday

What I have achieved this week:

What I have learned:

What I need to carry forward:

When the going gets tough

Aims

- To combat feelings of giving up.
- To use tough times to aid development.
- To focus on strengths and achievements.

Preparation

Have available a whiteboard or flipchart and copies of the handouts.

Introduction (5 minutes)

Discuss the aims for the session. State that everyone has good and bad days. There are times when things go well and other times when everything seems to be going wrong. Then we start thinking negatively and that the difficulties are too overwhelming to keep going. It is at these times that we need to step back, take stock, get things into perspective and do something to give ourselves a boost and help us overcome the difficulties being experienced.

Activity (20 minutes)

Give out Handout 1. Instruct participants to complete the 'Yes/No' and 'What you start thinking', part of the handout. Suggest they add any other triggers they experience which are not listed.

When completed ask individuals to pair up with a partner to discuss and complete the 'Changed attitude statement'. Before they start use the following example on the whiteboard or flipchart. Alternatively make one up of your own to demonstrate what is meant.

Trigger	Yes/No	What you start thinking	Changed attitude statement
When someone criticises you	Yes	She thinks I'm an idiot. I can't cope with this. I want to run away. I am stupid.	She's not criticising me. She's pointing out what went wrong and showing me how I can improve my performance. She will be pleased when I do it.

End the activity by getting volunteers to share a few examples – their trigger, what they start thinking and their changed attitude statement. Suggest everyone writes their proactive statements on a card so that they can take it out when an incident happens, read it and challenge their thinking.

Activity (20 minutes)

Explain that the aim of this activity is to help get the imagination to work when having difficulty finding any solutions to a problem. The mind has jammed and no new ideas are forthcoming and it seems a solution of any sort is impossible.

Sometimes it is best to stop thinking about the problem, do something that is enjoyable and relaxing such as going swimming, listening to music or getting on with something else. Hours or a day or so later when the mind returns to the problem ideas that have not been thought of begin to pop into mind. Some participants may have experienced this. Explain that this exercise uses the same technique but instead of leaving the problem for a night or longer it can enable a similar result in 15–20 minutes.

Ask everyone to think of something they really enjoy. This might be a place, a musical film, dancing, walking by a stream, listening to music, or smelling flowers. This is somewhere or an activity they can think about and feel absolutely relaxed as they imagine it. It is something they can escape to in their imagination – a 'haven' for total relaxation.

When everyone has conjured up and feels happy with their 'haven' instruct them to write down a problem that is worrying them and for which they have not been able to find a solution.

Now talk them through the process outlined in Handout 2.

When the process has been completed give out the handout and ask:

- How did doing that feel?
- Were you able to switch from relaxed mode in your 'haven' to thinking through the problem and back to relaxing again?
- Did any solutions come to mind?

State that practice is required to learn to use the method. It is in the switch over from relaxed mode to the problem that new ideas and thoughts most often occur. Also, it is best to practice ten or so minutes a day in a quiet place and time so there are no interruptions. Warn everyone that it is not a good idea to practice just before going to sleep as there is danger of drifting off thinking about the problem and thus tossing and turning worrying about it all night.

Closure (10 minutes)

Suggest that a good way to lift your spirits when feeling low and regain confidence and determination is to focus for a moment or two on strengths and past achievements. It helps get the current situation into proportion and reassure that difficulties can be overcome. Ask participants to imagine that they are writing an advert to sell themselves. This could be for the back cover of an autobiographical book. What strengths, skills and achievements would they include in their advertisement or blurb? Instruct them to quickly write down a list and then have a round of people stating their strengths and achievements.

Homework (5 minutes)

Direct participants to spend more time writing down their strengths and achievements on a card which they can then use as a constant reminder of their successes. They can also practice using their 'haven' as a problem solving method so that when they really need it they can use it automatically.

When the going gets tough: Handout 1

What triggers your feelings of discouragement and despair?

Trigger	Yes/No	What you start thinking	Changed attitude statement
When someone criticises you.			
Having to do a task you don't like.			
Needing to confront someone.			
When something goes wrong.			
When someone is angry with you.			
Needing to ask for help.			

Failing at something.	When you do not feel well.	Feeling ignored.	Losing out because of circumstances out of your control.	Not achieving what you thought possible.	**Other triggers**	

When the going gets tough: Handout 2

Kick-starting the imagination

Step 1:
Close your eyes, breathe deeply once or twice, and relax. Let the problem drift away out of mind. Think about your personal 'haven'. Bring it to mind in as much detail as possible. What can you see? What colour is it? What can you smell? What can you hear? Are you touching anything? What can you taste? Hold this for a moment or two.

Step 2:
Now focus on what the problem is? Think about it. How did it arise? Is it a barrier to what you want to achieve? In what way is it a barrier? What issues are involved? What are the difficulties? Who is involved or affected? Could they or anyone else help find a solution? Who? What are you feeling? What are your fears? Is it a problem because you will have to confront something you find difficult or unpleasant? Spend about two minutes focusing and exploring the problem. No longer than three minutes.

Step 3:
Now leave the problem behind again and retreat to your special place, protected from problems and worries. Allow the mind to relax and become absorbed in the surroundings of your 'haven'. Stay there for about two minutes totally relaxed and enjoying everything you see, touch, smell, hear and the beautiful colours.

Step 4:
Now focus on solutions to the problem. What do you want to achieve? What would be a good outcome? How could you make this happen? Are there different alternatives to choose from? What would be a first step? Focus on this for about two minutes. After two minutes list any solutions that have come to mind or ideas that could lead to some solutions.

Step 5:
Close your eyes again and step back into your 'haven'. Let your mind relax and rest again. Enjoy your surroundings. After a moment of relaxing, bring your ideas and solutions to mind. Envisage carrying them out and succeeding. Can you see and hear it happening? What does it feel like? Once you have visualised it open your eyes and orientate yourself to your surroundings again.

Emotional Development

- Understanding emotions
- Using communication styles to change feelings
- Emotional health and self-development through writing
- Using emotional communication skills

Understanding emotions

Aims

- To recognise and acknowledge emotions.
- To understand the purpose of emotions.
- To examine what happens when emotions are ignored or diverted.

Preparation

Have available copies of the handouts and a whiteboard or flipchart.

Introduction (15 minutes)

Present the aims for the session. Have the group members call out words which describe emotions they have experienced and write them on the board or flipchart. This may include:

- sad
- inferior
- worn out
- humiliated

- bored
- desperate
- comfortable
- ignored

- cheerful
- shocked
- vulnerable
- shy

- resentful
- wicked
- uptight
- stupid

When a long list has been written up on the board, choose a word and ask: 'How did you react physically to this feeling?'

Example answers from the word 'angry' might be: 'Tense shoulders. I had a headache. Trouble sleeping.' Answers from the word 'happy' might be: 'Relaxed. Had lots of energy. Felt at ease. Had a sense of wellbeing.'

After completing a few examples ask participants; 'Does what we feel and our physical reaction to those feelings tell us something?' For example, if someone feels 'anxious' and becomes tense and irritable this is an indication that something is wrong and action needs to be taken. If someone feels 'cheerful' and is energetic this is a good indication that everything is going well.

State that emotions we feel are neither good nor bad – they serve a purpose. We do need to pay close attention to them, acknowledge them, listen to the message they are telling us and take appropriate action.

Activity (15 minutes)

Give out Handout 1. Explain and discuss that something happens which gives rise to an emotion. If it is something that represents a gain to us then we are happy. This might be something achieved which builds our self-esteem and confidence and we feel more respected because of it.

If we interpret the event as something lost, this might be something we wanted to achieve, pride or mutual respect, we may feel angry because our values or sense of justice have been violated. We may feel afraid and anxious about the future if there is a loss of security. We may also feel sad because we have lost what we thought was a secure future or an achievement.

Ask participants if they can think of some examples they can share from their experience when they have felt:

- Anger because their values or sense of justice have been violated.
- Fear/anxiety/guilt because of something they did or has happened to them.
- Sadness from a sense of something lost.

Activity (15 minutes)

Explain that when confronted with painful or negative emotions we often put up defences to avoid dealing with them. Give out Handout 2 and ask participants to tick the boxes of any of the defences listed they use or have used to avoid uncomfortable or negative feelings.

When the task has been completed invite participants to share a few of the defences they have used and what the circumstances were. Did anyone include additional defences they use? Then ask the following questions and discuss:

- What is the outcome of using these types of defences?
- Does the problem get solved?
- There may be momentary relief but will you feel better in the long run?
- Do they distance you emotionally from other people?
- Do they stop you developing as a person?
- Is there a more appropriate way the feeling could have been dealt with?

Closure (10 minutes)

Write the following sentence beginnings up on the board or flipchart. Participants, in turn, complete the sentences.

'I learned that . . .'

'I was surprised that . . .'

Homework (5 minutes)

Instruct the group members to make notes in a diary or notebook about their emotional response to events, their physical reactions and any defensive actions they take to avoid dealing with them. (Other sessions can be used to enable participants to explore alternative methods of dealing with feelings).

Understanding emotions: Handout 1

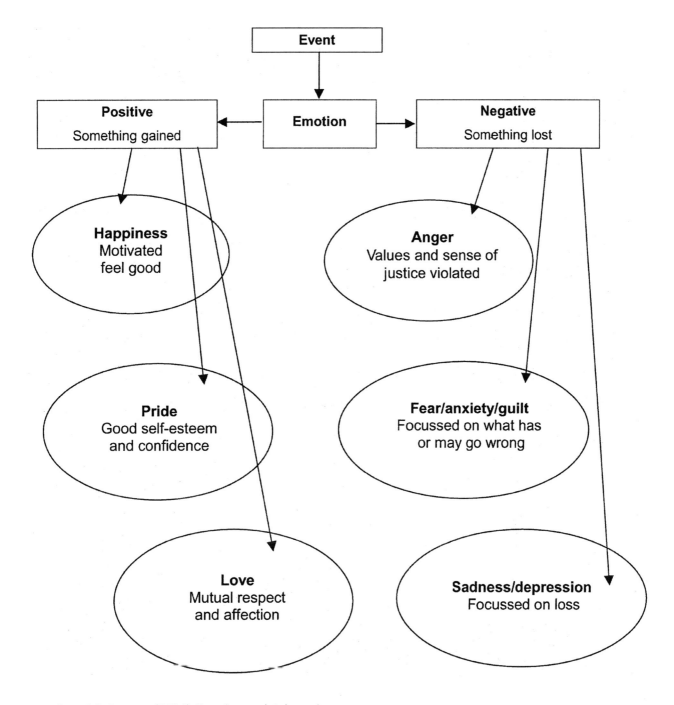

Based on R.S. Lazarus (1991) *Emotion and Adaptation*

Understanding emotions: Handout 2

Defences to avoid emotional pain

Defence action	Yes
Ignored a fear because you did not want to deal with it.	
Blocked out an emotion.	
Hoped to be rescued by someone or something.	
Blamed other people instead of accepting responsibility.	
Demanded complete obedience.	
Put someone down to feel better about yourself.	
Been inflexible.	
Did something to earn praise because you felt inadequate.	
Bragged about your accomplishments.	
Exaggerated your achievements.	
Faked it, making out what you wished was a reality.	
Ignored what you were being told or was obvious because you did not want to deal with something.	
Used excuses to avoid dealing with a painful event.	
Pretended everything was going well in spite of obvious setbacks.	
Criticised other people to keep them in their place.	
Been excessively neat and orderly to avoid feelings of not being in control or self-doubt.	
Pretended lack of understanding or created confusion and disorder to conceal the truth.	
Other defences I have used are:	

Using communication styles to change feelings

> **Aims**
>
> - To understand different styles of communication.
> - To identify personal styles.
> - To adjust your style to reduce feelings of anger, anxiety and sadness.
>
> **Preparation**
>
> Have available copies of the handouts.

Introduction (15 minutes)

Explain the aims for the session. State that there are four ways in which people tend to react and think when experiencing emotional feelings of anger, anxiety and sadness. Write the four reactions with a couple of example prompters underneath up on the whiteboard or flipchart as shown below:

1. Passive
   (helpless, apologetic)

2. Aggressive
   (arrogant, bossy)

3. Indirectly aggressive
   (sarcastic, deceitful)

4. Mutual respect
   (honest, direct)

Divide the group into four subgroups. Give out four pre-prepared large sheets of paper, each one headed with a different reaction type – one sheet to each subgroup. Ask them to write down all the words, phrases or sentences that describes the traits and thinking of someone reacting in that way.

End the activity with each group displaying their sheet and giving feedback on what they have written. Also, give out Handout 1.

Activity (15 minutes)

State that a person is most likely to communicate with someone else in a style that displays what they value most in that relationship:

1. Passive – they want to be liked.
2. Aggressive – they want to control the other person or triumph over them.
3. Mutual respect – they respect the other person and want to be treated in the same way.

Point out that while each of us may have a tendency to communicate in one style (for example: passive – want to be liked by everyone) we may act differently in different relationships.

Give out Handout 2. Go through the examples and provide an opportunity for participants to discuss anything they do not understand.

Next give out Handout 3 and ask the participants to complete the form for at least three current relationships.

Activity (15 minutes)

Ask group members to pair up with someone they have not worked with before. Each person now chooses one of the relationships they have written about on their handout and wants to change. They then discuss with their partner what they could do to change the relationship to help develop mutual respect and how they feel. Instruct them to make notes. Suggestions might include things like:

- 'Learn to say "no".'
- 'Use "I" statements. I would like . . .'
- 'Risk stating my opinion when asked for it.'
- 'Challenge my thinking. Do I really want to be better than her or do I just want to live a different sort of life, and make my own choices? Is she afraid of losing me?'

Closure (10 minutes)

Invite each participant, in turn, to state the relationship, the two communication styles and what they could do to change and improve the relationship.

Homework (5 minutes)

Instruct group members to experiment with the changes they have stated and record any changes they have in how they feel. They should also consider and record any changes in how they think the other person feels towards them.

Using communication styles to change feelings: Handout 1

Communication style	Traits
Passive	Tends to be dependent on others. Gives way to others. Clings to others. Needs lots of reassurance. Wants to be liked and everyone to be happy. Doesn't want to stir up emotional feelings in other people. Moans a lot. Acts helpless. Submissive. Always apologising.
Aggressive	Inflexible. Demands obedience. Very overbearing. Intolerant of others. Tries to control everyone. Afraid someone will take advantage. Often blames other people. Wants to be right about everything. Is opinionated. Very bossy.
Indirectly aggressive	Wants to be thought of as good or kind while thinking the opposite. Often is sarcastic. Expresses anger while trying to appear nice. Manipulates. Uses emotional blackmail. Insinuates things. Says one thing and does another. Is deceitful. Tries to get other people to express their anger.
Mutual respect	Acknowledges own feelings. Takes responsibility for own feelings. Thinks everyone has a right to their own feelings and to express them. Honest. Direct. Accepts and respects other people's feelings.

Using communication styles to change feelings: Handout 2

Name: Rita

Relationship	My communication style	The other person's communication style	The effect this has on the relationship and how you feel is:
Me – my mother	Aggressive – I want to show her I am better than her.	Aggressive – she wants to control me.	We are always arguing, falling out and upsetting each other.
Me – my boss	Passive – I want to be liked so I do everything I think she wants me to, even if I sometimes don't think it is right.	Mutual respect – she asks for my opinion and never takes me for granted.	I tend to accept what she says. I don't express my feelings when I disagree – even when she has asked me. I sometimes feel angry and used. My boss probably thinks I am not up to taking on more responsibility. I feel inadequate.
Me – my husband	Mutual respect.	Mutual respect.	We discuss things and tell each other what we are thinking. We are open and honest with each other. It feels good.

Using communication styles to change feelings: Handout 3

Name:

Relationship	My communication style	The other person's communication style	The effect this has on the relationship is:

Emotional health and self-development through writing

Aims

- To use writing to work through anger, fear and sadness.
- To use writing to plan for the future, set goals and build self-esteem.
- To practice using writing to achieve emotional health.

Preparation

Have available copies of the handouts, writing paper and pens and a whiteboard or flipchart.

Introduction (5 minutes)

Go through the aims for the session. Explain that expressing emotions by writing about them can bring about changes. It is like a boiler relieving pressure by letting out steam. As you write and express the emotions subtle changes occur. Somehow a switch is flipped creating a calming effect. You begin to realise things and make sense of what is happening. Writing about future worries can bring them back into perspective and clarify options from which to choose.

The beauty about private writing is that you do not have to show it to anyone – it can remain private. You can keep it or destroy it. That means you can drop all pretences and be honest.

Release is not always instant. Sometimes when writing about a sad experience you will feel sad but in a few days there is likely to be subtle changes happening. Your mood may be relieved or if you have written about a positive experience your self-esteem may have improved.

Activity (10 minutes)

Write one of the following sentence beginnings on the board or flipchart:

'I feel . . .'

'I miss . . .'

'I want . . .'

Ask each person to write a four line poem beginning each line with words on the board. Suggest they think of a relationship or situation and let it express their feeling about the relationship or situation. Examples are:

I feel needed	I feel tense
I feel loved	I feel uncomfortable
I feel irritated	I feel trapped
I feel tired	I feel guilt

When this has been completed ask if anyone has discovered anything about that relationship or situation or how they feel about it. If anyone wants to, invite them to read out their poem.

Activity (15 minutes)

Invite everyone to take part in a writing burst. That is, they quickly write down whatever comes into their head about something. They do not pay attention to spelling or grammar. Tell them no one is going to see or read it unless they want them to. They just write.

Write the words 'anger', 'fear' and 'sadness' on the board or a flipchart. Participants think of a current or recent experience in which they feel or felt anger, fear or sadness and write about it. They state what happened, how it felt emotionally and physically and what went through their mind. Suggest they use all the senses – feel, touch, smell, sight and taste – to write about it.

Write up on the board and suggest they also consider trying to answer some of the following questions:

- How do I feel?
- Why am I so upset, sad or angry?
- Is my upset, sadness or anger appropriate?
- What is the worst thing that could happen?
- What would I like to see happen?
- What can I do to solve the problem?
- What can I learn from this experience?

This will help them focus on using the process in a positive way rather than using it as a chance to complain and moan continuously about a situation, which would make them feel worse.

After about five to ten minutes stop everyone and ask:

- How did doing that feel?
- Were you able to express what you were feeling?
- Have you learned anything about the experience you were not aware of before?
- Do you think if you continued writing for longer the process would help you think through what happened?
- How do you feel now about the experience?

Activity (15 minutes)

This time write on the board:

- A good experience.
- How I want my life to be in five years time.
- Hopes for the future.
- Something I feel proud about.

Ask participants to choose one of the topics and write about it for five to ten minutes. When time is up ask the following:

- How did doing that feel?
- Were you able to express what you were feeling?

- Have you learned anything from writing about the experience you were not aware of before?
- How do you feel now? Has how you are feeling changed in any way from how you felt before you started writing?
- What effect do you think it would have if you wrote in a notebook regularly in this positive manner?

Closure (10 minutes)

Conduct a brainstorm on the board or flipchart of things that participants can write about regularly in their notebooks. Make it as long as possible in the time. Examples are provided in Handout 1. When completed give out Handout 1. Participants should also make notes from the board about topics they could write about.

Finally, remind participants that, if they have a computer, they can use a password to keep whatever they write about private. Also, that writing about upsetting events can reduce them and writing about positive or hopeful thoughts can increase them. Writing about future hopes and goals helps by focusing on personal desires, values and priorities and enables forward movement. Seeing the direction ahead makes it more likely that path will be taken.

Homework (5 minutes)

Suggest that everyone experiments with writing during the coming week. On at least four or five days they spend about fifteen minutes writing. If they run out of things to write they can repeat previous thoughts written about. They can choose to write about something that is upsetting them, joyful times or about their future, a combination or anything listed on Handout 1 or the board.

Once they have experimented with the process they can then decide how they want to use it. On a regular, daily or weekly basis or as and when needed to help with particular situations. To form the habit and to be able to do it automatically it is recommended that, initially, it is practiced on a regular basis.

Emotional health and self-development through writing: Handout 1

What I can write about:

- How I feel now
- My fears
- My goals
- Boundaries
- Things I want to do
- What if
- What is missing
- Things I feel proud about
- How others see me
- Love
- My beliefs
- When I feel sad
- Betrayal
- My age
- Absence
- My family
- Admiration
- Quiet moments
- Things I enjoy
- Things to celebrate
- Flowers
- Priorities

- Relationships
- Pain
- My values
- When I feel angry
- When I feel happy
- Shame
- My potential
- Joys
- My achievements
- Lies
- Shopping
- Failure
- Secrets
- Good times
- My best friend
- Beauty
- Anxieties
- What upsets me
- Honesty
- Challenges
- Things I am thankful for
- Change

Using emotional communication skills

Aims

- To increase ability to identify emotions.
- To practice emotional communication skills.
- To take responsibility for personal emotions.

Preparation

Have available copies of the handout and a whiteboard or flipchart. Also, cut out pictures from magazines depicting individuals showing different emotions. Number them on the back. Ten or twelve will be adequate.

Introduction (10 minutes)

Explain the aims for the session. State that it is important to be able to identify emotions in others and express it accurately ourselves. Ask participants:

- Why is it important? Ensure the answer includes:

  'Emotions are the best indicators to giving us a guide for what to do or say in different situations. For example: if your boss is in an angry mood it may not be the best time to ask for a favour. If your child comes home from school looking sad it indicates that something may be wrong. Also, if we express what we are feeling accurately we are more likely to get an appropriate response.'

- What happens when someone has too much control over their emotions and appears unemotional? How do we react?
- What happens when someone has little control over their emotions and is over-emotional? How do we react?
- Do people exercise the same emotional control in all types of situations? For example, in close personal relationships and in public. (*Emphasise that we can learn to moderate our emotional behaviour and expression – subdue expression, control temper so that they can be expressed at the right time and placed in appropriate and acceptable ways and in proportion to the event that has caused them.*)
- Do facial expressions of emotions differ across cultures? (*Expressions are universal across cultures (Emotions Revealed, Ekman, 2003). There may be differences in what is appropriate in where, when and the extent to which they are expressed.*)
- Do people sometimes mislead us with the expression and words they use? How? (*Smiling when they feel dreadful or want to mislead someone. Expressing one thing in words and miming something else.*)

Activity (5 minutes)

Do a quick brainstorm with the group and write on the whiteboard or flipchart words that express emotions. (See Handout 1.) Explain that we use these words and body language – facial expression, gesture and situation to indicate what we are feeling and to understand what other people are feeling.

Give out Handout 1.

Activity (15 minutes)

Pass the numbered pictures you have prepared around the class and have each participant write down what emotion they think is being expressed in the picture. Ask them not to tell each other their answers.

When everyone has had opportunity to write their answers down go through the list one by one to find out what answers people have given. Display each picture, in turn, while doing this. There will be different interpretations of many of the pictures. This is because many expressions are open to different interpretations. Point out that this indicates that when we think someone is expressing one thing it can be misinterpreted if we rely on expression alone.

Activity (15 minutes)

Each person, in turn, mimes an emotion – without speaking – they have chosen from the whiteboard, flipchart or Handout 1 and other members of the group try to guess what emotion they are miming. Again, many will be difficult to interpret correctly. Some group members will disagree on interpretations. This emphasises the need to learn appropriate expressions to show what we feel and to use words as well.

Closure (10 minutes)

Explain that what we feel is our own responsibility. We must accept responsibility for it and not blame other people and events – even though it may have been an action by the other person or an event that has resulted in our feeling. A good way of doing this is to think in or make 'I feel' statements. For example: 'I feel humiliated and get angry when you criticise me in front of your mother. I want you to stop doing it.' Doing this avoids blaming the other person for how you feel, lets them know what you feel and tells them what you want them to do about it. The same principle applies to positive events. For example: 'I enjoyed our discussion. I feel much more confident about the project. I would like to do this again in a months' time. Is that possible?'

Ask group members to think of an incident when they have felt an emotion – perhaps one chosen from the board – and make an 'I' statement about it.

Homework (5 minutes)

Instruct participants to check out their emotional communication skills. Do their expressions and body language match what they are saying? Suggest they practice using expressions in a mirror. Are they interpreting other people's emotions correctly? They can check by asking the other person. For example: 'You said you were OK but you look sad? Is something wrong?' Or, 'I think I may have confused you. Would you like me to explain what to do in a different way?'

They can also practice using 'I feel . . .' statements.

Ekman, P. (2003) *Emotions Revealed*. Weidenfeld and Nicolson.

Using emotional communication skills: Handout 1

anger	boredom	sadness
anxiety	determination	happiness
joy	loneliness	shock
annoyance	surprise	enthusiasm
irritation	envy	jealousy
relief	guilt	suspicion
disgust	caution	puzzlement
concern	worry	fear
panic	surprise	depression
fury	offence	shyness
sympathy	agony	helplessness
apathy	bitterness	confidence
pride	discouragement	friendliness
embarrassment	hate	indifference
excitement	scorn	repulsion
hope	pity	exhaustion
inadequate	numbness	confusion
optimistic	superiority	stress
negative	calm	exasperation

Harnessing Creativity

- Releasing your creativity
- Creative thinking
- Don't live with it: improve it!
- Promoting your creativity

Releasing your creativity

Aims

- To stimulate personal creativity.
- To encourage thinking out of the box.
- To apply creative thinking to everyday life.

Preparation

Have available copies of the handouts and a whiteboard or flipchart.

Introduction (15 minutes)

Outline the aims for the session. Give out Handout 1 and explain that sometimes we have a tendency to think with the left side of our brain – that is using logic, analysis and placing everything in sequence. At other times we use the right side of the brain – that allows us to let our imagination free, daydream and think of lots of new ideas. For example, when we freely brainstorm all sorts of ideas, many of the ideas may at first seem outrageous, silly and far-fetched. We do not worry about that but let our imagination have free flow, forgetting logic, sequence, analysis etc. Once we have lots of ideas we can then bring the right side of our brain into action to work out which idea has potential and to make it work. In order to carry out this creative act we first need to learn to let the right (creative) side of our brain free to work and not be restricted by the left (logical) side. Some people restrict their creativity by over use of the logical side of their brain.

State that you now want everyone to do a short exercise using the creative side of their brain. Give out Handout 2. Do an example on the board. You can make one up for yourself or use the following:

- My name is a *restricted area*.
- I taste like *bitter lemon*.
- I smell like *seaweed*.
- I feel like *a caged bird*.
- I sound like *a high pitched violin*.
- I look like *a neatly trimmed hedge*.

Instruct participants to complete the handout letting their imagination free to describe themselves in this way. When they have completed the task ask them, in turn or randomly, to read out their personal descriptions. Next ask them how they felt doing the exercise. Did anyone feel uncomfortable? Explain that using the right side of their brain will, at times, feel uncomfortable – especially until they get used to letting their creativity have its freedom.

Activity (10 minutes)

Write on the whiteboard or flipchart: 'Being creative is . . .' Ask participants to make suggestions about what they think is meant by saying someone is creative. Write the suggestions on the board. See if the group can arrive at a definition of what 'being creative' means.

Next ask: 'What sort of things can we use our creativity for?'

Answers might include things like:

Cooking	Writing stories	Gardening
Planning outings	Decorating a room	Playing a sport
Housework	Letter writing	Arranging a work space
Flower arranging	Photography	Solving problems
Training pets	Organising a party	Composing music
Relationships	How to get a job	Problems

Activity (20 minutes)

Give out Handout 3. Listed are some of the thinking barriers that stop people being creative. Instruct them to first rate themselves on how often they use the sort of thinking listed to block creativity. A different pattern will emerge for each person. When completed give an opportunity for individuals to comment on their results and the effect this has on them being creative.

Now go through each barrier listed, working as a group, and fill in more positive ways to substitute for the negative thinking listed that will help activate creative thinking. By the end of the activity everyone should have a range of 'creative thinking activator' thoughts they can use when they catch themselves using the 'creative thinking barriers'.

Closure (10 minutes)

Give out Handout 4. Ask the participants to complete it. When they have done this ask for volunteers to share their decisions.

Homework (5 minutes)

Ask the participants to keep a diary of how often they catch themselves using the 'barriers to creative thinking' and substitute 'creative thinking activator' thoughts and what effect this has. Also instruct them to start applying creative thinking to the tasks they have chosen.

Releasing your creativity: Handout 1

Right-brain   **Left-brain**

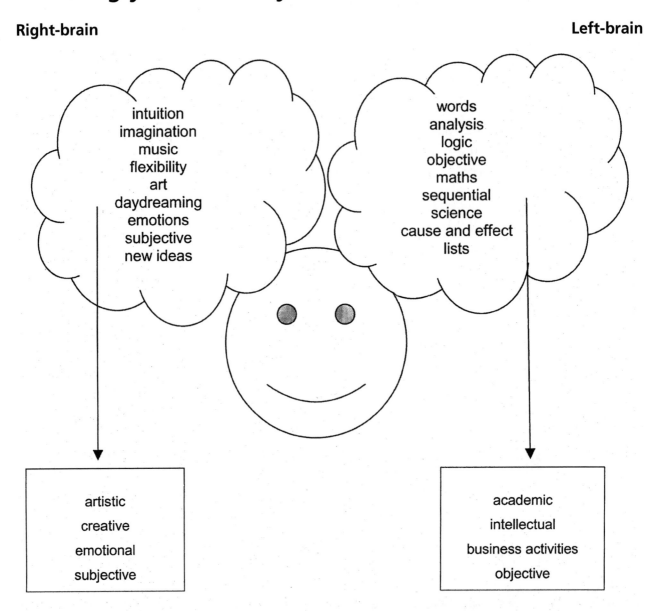

intuition
imagination
music
flexibility
art
daydreaming
emotions
subjective
new ideas

words
analysis
logic
objective
maths
sequential
science
cause and effect
lists

artistic

creative

emotional

subjective

academic

intellectual

business activities

objective

Creative potential is greatest when you use both sides of your brain.

Releasing your creativity: Handout 2

My name is

_____

I taste like

_____

I smell like

_____

I feel like

_____

I sound like

_____

I look like

_____

Releasing your creativity: Handout 3

Creative thinking barriers	Never	Sometimes	Often	Creative thinking activators
Time – "I'm too busy and have no time to be creative.'				(Example: 'If I think creatively about this I can actually save time.')
Fear of risk taking – 'Being creative means trying out new ideas. What if they do not work? I'll look foolish.'				
Perfectionism – 'Everything has to be perfect in every way. It isn't worth doing unless it is.'				
Black and white thinking – 'There is only one way to do things. I feel uncomfortable if that is not followed.'				
Uncreative self-talk – "I'm just not creative. I've never been good at that sort of thing. My family always told me so.'				
Dismissing creativity – 'It's wasteful. It's not logical, nor does it make any sense.'				

Poor environment – 'When things are better I will be creative. At the moment I have limited resources.'	**Blinkered thinking** – 'There is only one answer or way to do this.'	**Don't rock the boat** – 'Making changes will cause upheaval and might upset things. It's best to do what we have always done.'

Releasing your creativity: Handout 4

Things in my life I can apply creative thinking to are:

1

2

3

4

I will do this: (when?)	(where?)
1	1
2	2
3	3
4	4

Creative thinking barriers I will challenge are:

1

2

3

4

Creative thinking

Aims

- To practice generating new ideas.
- To show how easy it is to react negatively to new ideas.
- To create a criteria to help decide which ideas to use.

Preparation

Have available copies of the handouts, a twelve inch ruler or other object, flipchart sheets and magic markers.

Introduction (10 minutes)

Explain the aims for the session. Show a twelve-inch ruler to the group. Ask group members to think of something it can be used for apart from measuring or drawing lines. Pass it round and have each person state and demonstrate the use they have in mind. Go round the group twice. Suggestions may include:

shoe horn	book mark	scraper
back scratcher	baton	drawer divider
fly swat	catapult	cake mixer
pendulum	prop	drumstick

When the rounds have been completed state that the group has just used their imagination to generate lots of ideas and think creatively. They can use the same fun method to solve problems that they encounter in life.

Activity (10 minutes)

Form the participants into three sub-groups. Give each sub-group a flipchart sheet, a magic marker and one of the topics cut out from a photocopy of Handout 1. Alternatively, make up subjects you can use that are more likely to be encountered by the group members. Give the subgroups about five minutes to come up with as many ideas as possible to solve the problem or answer the question.

End the activity by having each subgroup share their ideas for their question?

Activity (15 minutes)

Divide the participants into two subgroups and give each group two new flipchart sheets – one sheet headed 'positive' and the other 'negative'. Ask each subgroup member to think back to when they had a new idea or a change they wanted to make. This might have been at work or at home, perhaps even a change of routine or what to do.

First ask them to think of all the negative responses they had to their new ideas or changes proposed and write them down on the 'negative' sheet. When complete instruct them to think about all the positive comments and responses they remember being made and write these down on the 'positive' sheet.

Complete the exercise by totalling the number of 'negative' responses from both subgroups. Also, total the 'positive' comments and responses.

Most groups will have found it easier to come up with negative responses to new ideas and change – often dismissing them as impossible or as too much bother. This is because most of us have been conditioned to receive and give negative responses and so tend to give less consideration to the positive side of new ideas or changes. Ask the group members what effect they think this has on what we do, how we live and respond to new ideas and change.

Activity (15 minutes)

Having come up with new ideas or changes to achieve what we want the next stage requires us to decide on what idea or combination of ideas to use. One way to do this is to set down some sort of criteria. That means looking at what is most important in this particular circumstance to achieve what we want. Give out Handout 2 and briefly discuss the example given.

Reform the three subgroups as in the earlier activity. Give a copy of Handout 3 to each subgroup and instruct them to set down a criteria list for the subject they generated ideas about. They then decide which idea or combination of ideas best fits the criteria.

Closure (5 minutes)

Briefly discuss how each subgroup got on with their task. Ask:

- What criteria did they set?
- Was deciding the criteria difficult?
- Did it help decide what idea or combination of ideas to use?
- How useful do they think they would find using the process in real life?
- Can they think of a problem or situation in which they might use it?

Homework (5 minutes)

Instruct the participants to apply the method of creative thinking to a problem or something they would like to do in the coming week.

Creative thinking: Handout 1

What could you do if you were being bullied by your boss?

What could you do if your partner went missing while you were on holiday?

What could you do to reduce your living costs if you were in debt?

What could you do if you came across two neighbours having an argument?

What could you do to prepare yourself for a job interview?

What could you do if you were made homeless?

What could you do if you wanted to avoid mixing with a group of people who were a bad influence on you?

Creative thinking: Handout 2

Topic. What could you do if you were asked to prepare activities to occupy a group of children for a day?

The most important things in preparing activities for this group of children for a day are:

---

1. Ensuring health and safety.

2. Making sure the activities will be enjoyed by everyone.

3. Providing something which aids their learning and development.

4. Doing something which produces an end product for them to take away.

5. Providing something active which gives an outlet for their high energy levels.

6. The activities must suit or be adaptable to the limited space in the room provided.

Creative thinking: Handout 3

Topic.

The most important things are:

The idea or combination of ideas which best meets the above criteria are:

Don't live with it: improve it!

Aims

- To motivate participants to use their creativity to improve their situations.
- To raise awareness of how creativity can be used in everyday life.
- To practice using creativity to improve personal situations.

Preparation

Have available copies of the handouts, a plain brown or white box and a whiteboard or flipchart.

Introduction (15 minutes)

Discuss the aims for the session. State that being creative involves taking risks, doing things differently, making mistakes, learning from experience and persevering. Ask group members to think of something new they have tried to do in the past, a problem they have attempted to solve or a mistake they have made and what they have learned from it. Write one or two examples on the whiteboard or flipchart. Examples might be:

What I tried to do	What I learned
Cook a meal for my partner and the family.	How much effort goes into making a successful meal and how hard my partner works.
Challenge my partner about clearing up after himself in front of his mother.	Not to criticise my partner in front of his mother but approach the subject when on our own.
Grow a sunflower.	It needs to be carefully placed in a sunny spot, to be supported so the stem does not break and requires lots of water and care.

After a moment or two for thought ask each participants, in turn, to state something new they tried to do, a problem they attempted to solve or a mistake they made and what they learned from it.

When the statements have been made ask and discuss:

- What does their experiences show about the value of taking risks, attempting something new and making mistakes?

110

- Do people feel reluctant about sharing mistakes they make? Why? What is the value in sharing mistakes?
- What does their shared experience tell them about creativity, how they learn and develop and perseverance?

Activity (15 minutes)

State that creative thinkers question everyday things, identify problems and use their creative imagination to improve them. This applies to both things and situations. What creative thinkers ask themselves is; 'How can this object or situation be improved . . .'

Pass a plain cardboard box – can be brown or white and any size – around the group members for them to examine. Tell them that you are a dispatch manager and have been sending delicate glass objects through the post in the boxes but they keep being returned with the box crushed and the objects broken. Also, there have been comments that the box looks tatty, unattractive and does not present a good image for the company you work for. Now work with the group to come up with a better designed box, that is attractive and in which the glass objects can safely be delivered. Writing on the whiteboard, use the process shown in Handout 1 to do this.

When the example has been completed on the board, state that this is what creative people do, ask questions to establish what needs to be improved, look at different ways to improve it and then try out what they think is the best method to do so. This applies to practical things like the example, situations we find ourselves in, relationships we want to improve and how we live out lives.

Activity (15 minutes)

Give out Handout 1. Ask participants to close their eyes and examine different areas of their lives. This could be work, their home life, their social life, relationships, a situation, a place they live or something they do. Can they spot something that they think could be improved to make life more satisfying? This might be improvements to:

- A relationship
- Relaxation time
- A work environment
- Carrying out a regular chore
- A bedroom

After a moment or two for thought instruct everyone to complete the 'What I want to improve . . .' and 'The problem with this is . . .' sections of the handout. When completed have them work in pairs to complete the 'Ideas to improve this are . . .' section. Each person then chooses what ideas or combination of ideas they will use to make the improvements.

Closure (10 minutes)

Facilitate a short discussion on what has been learned. Write participants' statements on the whiteboard or flipchart. Prompt by asking:

- Should they fear making mistakes when attempting something new? Why not?

- Do people, from time to time, look at what they can improve in their lives or do they just live with uncomfortable situations?
- Should they give up when they make mistakes? Why not?

Homework (5 minutes)

Have participants state what they have chosen to improve, how and when they intend doing this. Instruct them to carry out the action they have decided. Point out how carrying out their actions will build their confidence in the method, so they can use this creative approach for any areas of their lives they want to improve.

Don't live with it: improve it! Handout 1

What I want to improve is:

The problem with this is:

Ideas to improve it are:

What I am going to do to improve it is:

Promoting your creativity

Aims

- To understand the necessity to promote new ideas.
- To learn how to describe the advantages of an idea.
- To practice promoting an idea.

Preparation

Have available copies of the handout and a whiteboard or flipchart.

Introduction (15 minutes)

Go through the aims for the session. Ask if anyone has ever proposed what they thought was a good idea at work, at home or to friends and had it ignored or scorned. How did they feel? State that sometimes people have good creative ideas but they are brushed aside or ignored. The person who proposed the idea can feel isolated; that their creativity is no good or that there is little point if others do not listen. To counteract this we all need to acquire skills in selling our ideas to colleagues at work and friends and family who will be affected by them.

Ask participants: *'Why do people resist new ideas?'*

Write the comments on the whiteboard or flipchart and discuss. This should include:

- The idea is not understood.
- They don't see any advantage in it for them.
- Dislike of change.
- They can not visualise or see it in practice.
- They do not think it would work.
- It doesn't fit how they see things.
- They don't see why change is necessary.
- They are in a rut.
- They don't see the relevance.
- It does not seem new or novel.
- Not presented with enough enthusiasm.
- Does not seem credible.

Activity (15 minutes)

Give out Handout 1. Instruct each participant to think of an idea they have had and want to initiate. They can choose something to do with work, home or their social life. It might be where to go for an outing or a holiday, how they might overcome a problem at home, that they should decorate a bedroom and so on. When they have decided on something they then use Handout 1 to describe their idea and what the benefits will be with a view to persuading whoever else is involved that it is a good idea and getting their support.

Activity (15 minutes)

Have the participants form pairs and take turns, using their notes, role-playing the scenarios to persuade each other that their idea is a good one. They then give each other feedback on how well they have done and what might have helped them be more persuasive. If there is time they can form a second pairing and receive more feedback and practice.

Closure (10 minutes)

Facilitate a discussion on the activity. Prompt by asking:

- How did they feel doing the role-play?
- How persuasive were the presentations of the ideas?
- What did they learn that will be helpful in the future?
- What did they discover they needed to do better?
- Would more time to think the issues through have helped?
- In real life do they take time to think the issues through so they can promote their ideas?
- What was difficult?
- What was easy?

Homework (5 minutes)

Ask participants how they now feel about presenting their idea to the other person or persons involved. Discuss any identified difficulties and instruct them to go ahead and present their idea in the coming week. Point out that every idea is unlikely be accepted but, having thought it through and paid attention to the issues for other people, the chances of acceptance is much greater.

Promoting your creativity: Handout 1

Description of the idea. Use simple words and sentences. Say why it is necessary or desirable and why you are enthusiastic about it.

My idea is

Benefits and advantages. Include how it will benefit anyone else involved.

Checklist. I have taken into account as appropriate: (add all the things listed on the whiteboard)

- Advantages for other people affected.
- Making it credible.
- Making it workable.
- Believing in it and being enthusiastic.

- How other people might see it.
- Why change is necessary/helpful.
- Making it relevant.
- Helping others to visualise it happening.

Life Management Skills

- Rules for living
- Marketing your strengths and skills
- Learning to negotiate
- Keeping records

Rules for living

Aims

- To examine why rules are needed.
- To explore the consequences of breaking rules.
- To discuss what happens when a rule is unfair or becomes outdated.

Preparation

Have available copies of the handouts, some flipchart sheets, magic markers and a whiteboard or flipchart.

Introduction (15 minutes)

Go through the aims for the session. Ask and briefly discuss:

- What is meant by the word 'rules'?
- Why is it important to have rules?
- Are some rules negotiable and others not? Why is this?
- What would it be like without rules?
- Are 'rules' always 'right' or 'fair'? Why not?

Invite the group members to brainstorm a list of rules. Remind them about the ground rules agreed when you formed the group. Write the suggestions on the whiteboard or flipchart. Try to ensure a range of personal and general rules encountered. Examples might include:

- No parking
- Speed limits
- Keep off the grass
- Be in by ten o'clock

- No smoking
- Contract of employment
- Respect confidentiality
- No loud music after ten o'clock

Ask and discuss:

- Are all rules written down?
- What types of rules are not written down?
- What is the consequence if you break the law?
- What are the consequences if you break unwritten rules?
- Are some rules negotiable and some not? Which?

Quickly brainstorm aspects of life which have rules. This might include:

- clubs
- councils
- employers
- families
- games
- classes
- parks
- restaurants
- drivers
- friends
- tenants
- societies
- governments
- schools
- groups
- public buildings

Complete the activity by asking if anyone admits to breaking any rules. What was the consequence?

Activity (30 minutes)

Divide the participants into three sub-groups. Give each sub-group some flipchart sheets and magic markers to record their results. Provide each sub-group with one of the tasks in Handout 1 or make up three situations suited to the group members' situations. Suggest that, when carrying out the tasks, different group members argue the viewpoint of different people involved in the situations. How would they feel about the rules? Are they likely to keep to them?

After a set time – about 15–20 minutes – have each sub-group present their findings. When they have done so ask:

- How easy or difficult was the process?
- What were the issues and difficulties?

Closure (10 minutes)

Give out Handout 2 and ask participants to think about an aspect of their lives where:

1. They have not agreed a rule and think there should be one.
2. They think the rules are unfair.
3. The rules have become outdated, are no longer useful and need renegotiating.

This may be in:

- A personal relationship. For example, how money is spent, behaviour that is unacceptable or how time is spent together.
- A club or society that they belong to where rules need to be introduced or changed to deal with an issue.
- An issue at work that requires a rule or a change to suit new circumstances.

Ask them to complete the handout for at least two issues or rules they would like to see changed.

Homework (5 minutes)

Invite participants to state one issue they have recorded on Handout 2 and think should have a rule or a rule that they think should be changed or renegotiated. Finish by instructing them to carry out their plan.

Rules for living: Handout 1

Group task

Imagine you are a family on holiday in a foreign country – Mum, Dad, a 15 year old daughter who looks about 18 and a 19 year old son who constantly gets into trouble. Your daughter has met a boy who is 17 and who invites her to join him and few other friends on a trip to a local island for a day. She is adamant she wants to go. Your son has taken up with a group of locals and wants to go with them to a beach party. He has, on a previous night, got drunk with some other lads staying in your hotel and got into an argument. You want him to enjoy himself and are pleased he has made some friends but are afraid, if alcohol is available, he will do the same thing again.

Discuss and state how would you go about agreeing rules for the rest of the holiday.

What rules might apply?

Would the rules be the same for both your daughter and son?

If not, why not?

How would you ensure any rules were adhered to?

What consequences would there be if the rules were broken?

Group task

You have a small business that both you and your partner started together. Up to now you have not needed any staff but now you have obtained a contract which means you will have to take on some employees.

Discuss and state what rules might you impose.

Why?

How would you decide on the rules?

What consequences, if any, would you impose if the rules were broken?

Group task

You have met a person whom you rate romantically. You have gone out together a few times. You really like the person and want to establish a long-term relationship.

Discuss and state what rules might come into play.

How would you ensure that you both had the same understanding of how to behave?

Would there be any rules?

How would you agree them?

How would you ensure they were adhered to?

What consequences would there be if the rules were broken?

Rules for living: Handout 2

Issues that require rules to be agreed, renegotiated or changed are:	Consequences if this does not happen are:	People who need to be involved in deciding the rules are:	To achieve this I can:	I will do this: (state when)

Marketing your strengths and skills

> ## Aims
>
> - To recognise personal strengths and skills.
> - To match strengths and skills to an objective or goal.
> - To practice selling yourself in a safe environment.
>
> ## Preparation
>
> Have available copies of the handout, a whiteboard or flipchart, large sheets of paper, coloured pens, a selection of magazines and newspapers, scissors and glue.

Introduction (10 minutes)

Discuss the aims for the session. Explain that being able to market yourself entails being aware of the skills and strengths you have to contribute to, or advance, a situation. This might include persuading someone to invest time or money or take a risk on you. It might be to pursue a goal, develop an idea, obtain a job or do something. The challenge in doing this is to match the strengths and skills you have to offer with what is needed to do the job or achieve the goal and present yourself in an appropriate way. You need to become your own spin doctor.

State that people often feel uncomfortable and embarrassed when speaking about their good points. To practice doing this, invite each person, in turn, to state their name and a strength or skill they have that they could sell. This might be anything from being a good cook or driver to having a good imagination or ability to respond well under pressure.

Activity (10 minutes)

Give out advertisements cut from magazines and newspapers. State that adverts are used in a number of ways: (write on the whiteboard or flipchart)

- To show goods or service advantages
- To project an image of the company, goods or service
- To provide essential information

Now using the adverts given out as examples, discuss how they do this. Include:

- Uses of colour, pictures, drawings, bold printing etc.
- Statements about what the product or service will do for the buyer.
- How the advert gets the benefits across to the reader.
- How the advert matches the needs and requirements of the readers.

Activity (25 minutes)

Ask participants to think of a job, an ambition, a goal or something they want to do. This might be to organise something like a family or works outing, apply for a particular type of job or do something for charity etc. Give out some large sheets of paper, coloured pens, a selection of magazines and newspapers, scissors and glue. Now instruct participants, working in pairs, to design their own advertisement displaying their strengths, skills and abilities to achieve what they want to do and match the requirements of whoever they are doing it for – the family, colleagues, a perspective employer, etc. Give out Handout 1. Suggest they use sections 1 to 5 when working in pairs to generate ideas and decide on what should be prioritised in their adverts. They then proceed to use the materials – writing, drawing, cutting out pictures etc – provided to design their advert.

Closure (10 minutes)

Ask each person, in turn, to display their advert and state what they wanted to do. Other group members ask questions, state how appealing they find the advert and make suggestions about how the person might have better sold themselves to meet the need of the people that the advert is selling to. These comments can be noted in section 6 of Handout 1.

Homework (5 minutes)

Ask participants to think of something they need to sell to someone. This might be what they have worked on in the activities or something different. Examples might be to sell their ability to do a particular task or take on extra responsibility at work to their manager, to become a committee member of a club, to organise a party, to look after a younger sister or grandmother when Mum and Dad are away for a weekend, to decorate your own room or look after a neighbour's garden and so on. Instruct participants to use Handout 1 to think through the process to decide how they are going to sell themselves and then do it. After they have put it into practice they can then record any ways they think they could sell themselves better next time.

Marketing your strengths and skills: Handout 1

1. What I want to do is:

2. My strengths, skills, experience and ability to do this include:

3. To match the needs of my audience my advert should include:	4. My reason is:

5. What I need to emphasise is:

6. Ways I could have sold myself better are:

Learning to negotiate

Aims

- To consider different styles of negotiation.
- To apply negotiation skills to personal situations.
- To practice using negotiation skills.

Preparation

Have available a whiteboard or flipchart, some coins or bars of chocolate and copies of the handout.

Introduction (5 minutes)

Explain the aims for the session. State that negotiation and bartering is a part of everyday life. Ask participants for examples of things about which they might negotiate or barter. This might include things like:

- Negotiating a discount on a TV.
- Exchanging one thing for another.
- Taking turns doing something.
- How much to pay back each week of a loan.
- How much you will get paid for doing a job.
- Who will do what on a committee.
- Help when feeling stressed.

Activity (10 minutes)

Split the group into pairs. Give each pair a coin or bar of chocolate. Tell them they have a few minutes to decide between them who is going to get and keep the coin or bar of chocolate. If they cannot reach a decision the coin or bar of chocolate must be returned to you. No physical force or touching is allowed. If someone decides to allow the other person to have the coin or chocolate bar they must try to obtain something from them in return.

- Stop the activity after a few minutes and discuss:
- What methods did people use to try to get the prize?
- What did they trade in order to have it?
- Did everyone play fair?

Activity (10 minutes)

Give out Handout 1. Ask individuals to think of something that they want. This might be a few hours off work, a sister to baby sit, a reduction in rent, someone to decorate your bedroom, a pay rise, someone to help with the amount of work you have to do and so on. They write this in the 'What I want' section of the handout. Suggest they consider their work, personal and family situation when thinking about what they want.

Next they think of what they have to offer in return for this and write this down in the 'What I can offer' section. Suggest they try to think of things that might appeal to and be of value to the other person. This might include doing some gardening for them, help with homework assignments, cooking meals for them, taking on extra responsibility, driving them somewhere and so on. Encourage people to list as many things as possible that could be traded.

Activity (15 minutes)

Now, working with different partners to the earlier activity, instruct participants to role play the situations. Individuals explain their situation to their partners. For example, an employee wanting a pay rise from their boss. Their partner takes the role of being their boss who is reluctant to agree and the negotiations begin. When agreement has been reached they record the outcome on 'What I have agreed', 'What I offered' sections of Handout 1. They also record what they feel are the benefits of this arrangement.

Closure (15 minutes)

Ask and discuss the following:

- Who was aggressive?
- Who was passive?
- Who was cooperative?
- Who was uncooperative?
- Is this style of negotiating typical of you?
- Should different styles be used for different situations?
- What did you learn about negotiating?
- Who got good deals?
- Were there things you did not consider but might now?
- What did you learn about yourself?
- What could you do to strengthen your ability to negotiate?

Homework (5 minutes)

Discuss any difficulties they think they might have in carrying out this negotiation for real and instruct them to think through what they have to offer again and carry through their plan.

Learning to negotiate: Handout 1

Name:

What I want	What I can offer
What I have agreed to accept	**What I have offered**

Benefits of this arrangement are:

Keeping records

Aims

- To recognise the value of keeping records.
- To be able to present a range of evidence to demonstrate abilities.
- To begin putting together a portfolio.

Preparation

Have available copies of the handouts, a whiteboard or flipchart and, if possible, a mock-up portfolio with examples of evidence.

Introduction (15 minutes)

Present the aims for the session. Ask participants what records they keep as part of everyday life and list on the board or flipchart. This might include:

- A personal diary
- Video of a wedding or other event
- Addresses and telephone numbers
- Examination and award certificates
- A weight chart
- Bank and spending record
- References
- Reports on work performance
- Newspaper cuttings of achievements
- Customer comments
- Examples of work
- Photographs

Now ask: 'Why keep records?' List the answers on the board or flipchart. Example answers are:

- Something to look back on.
- To remind me of what I have done.
- To check things.
- To prove what I have achieved.
- To help me see what skills I want to develop.
- To get promotion.
- To apply for a course of learning.
- To change jobs.
- To remind myself of what I am capable and build confidence.
- To plan what I want to do next.
- To help me complete application forms for jobs.

- To share with other people.
- To get recognition for an achievement.
- To get voluntary work.

Explain that it is necessary to keep a portfolio as a record for these reasons. Once we have accumulated enough information in it we can then take appropriate bits out of it to do any of these things.

Activity (15 minutes)

Give out Handout 1. Instruct individuals to choose something they are good at or can do and complete Handout 1 as shown in the example. Finish by inviting participants to share what they are good at and what they can use as evidence. Other group member may be able to suggest ideas that individuals have not thought about.

Activity (15 minutes)

State that a portfolio should contain:

- A curriculum vitae at the front
- A list of strengths and skills
- Evidence that proves or demonstrates achievements, strengths and skills.

State that to start a portfolio the first step is to compile a curriculum vitae. Give out Handout 3 as an example and answer any questions regarding putting a CV together. Give out Handout 4 and start participants working on and writing down what they could include in their CV. Suggest that when they have decided what they want to go in it they type or get it typed up. It is helpful to pass around a completed portfolio for them to see if you have one available.

Explain that once they have got their CV completed they can then start thinking about how they can provide evidence for everything in it using copies of Handout 2. It is a good idea to work backwards in time. This evidence can then be included as part of their portfolios.

Give out Handout 5. State that the list of strengths and skills can be compiled using the abilities required to do what has been listed in the CV.

Stop the activity after an allotted time and point out that putting the portfolio together will take effort and time. They will need to set time aside to do it.

Closure (10 minutes)

Ask participants:

- How they feel about completing the task.
- What have they learned by discussing and starting to carry out this task.
- Have they thought of any achievements they had forgotten about?
- Has anything occurred to them that they had not previously thought of that they can record as achievements or strengths?
- Is this a useful way to record their experiences, strengths and achievements?

- What uses will they get from it when it has been completed and is up to date?
- Once completed, how difficult will it be to keep it up to date?

Homework (5 minutes)

Instruct participants to set time aside to put their portfolios together. Answer any questions or queries and clarify anything that has not been understood.

Keeping records: Handout 1

Example

I am good at:	My experience includes:	Evidence I can use to prove this is:
Designing jewellery	Entered design competition. Did a college course. Worked for 3 years for . . . Put on an exhibition at local art centre. Sell my own jewellery.	2nd prize certificate. Award certificate. Reference. Newspaper cuttings and photographs. Letters of satisfaction from customers and examples of work.

I am good at:	My experience includes:	Evidence I can use to prove this is:

Keeping records: Handout 2

I am good at:	My experience includes:	Evidence I can use to prove this includes:

I am good at:	My experience includes:	Evidence I can use to prove this includes:

I am good at:	My experience includes:	Evidence I can use to prove this includes:

Keeping records: Handout 3

Joan Smith Curriculum Vitae

Personal details

Name: Joan Smith

Address: 38 Malcolm Crescent
Good Street
Pinkton
CH14 9AB

Telephone No: (01304) 968432

Date of birth: (1.9.71)

Education and training

Dates	Schools	Qualifications
1975–1981	Old Street Primary School Pinkton	
1981–1986	Magna Secondary School Princess Street Pinkton	CSE English and Maths
1999–2000	Pinkton Adult Learning The Grange Monkton Road Pinkton	NVQ Level 2 Hairdressing

Employment

Dates	Employer	Job Title	Responsibilities and duties
1986–1989	Shore Delivery Services Langdon Road Pinkton	Admin Assistant	Filing Booking deliveries in and out Typing letters Doing the post Answering phone queries Reception
1989–1995	Unemployed (At home caring for young child)		

1995–1999	QA Department Store Market Street Pinkton	Sales assistant	Serving customers Replacing sold stock Displaying stock Taking payment Providing information about goods Stocktaking Demonstrating beauty products
1999–2002	QA Department Store Market Street Pinkton	Hairdresser	Booking appointments Shampooing Cutting and colouring Doing perms
2002–2008	Scissors Beauty Salon High Street Pinkton	Manager	Managing 3 staff Responsible for day-to-day running of the salon.

Voluntary activities

Dates	Organisation	Job title	Responsibilities and duties
1991–2000	Portland Learning Disability Club	Volunteer Assistant	Providing activities for club members. Serving meals. Ensuring a safe environment for club members.
2002–2008	Pinkton Adult Learning The Grange Monkton Road Pinkton	Linking volunteer	Picking up disabled or vulnerable learners at their home, transporting them to a course of learning, supporting them in class and take them home again.

Interests
Member of Pinkton library music appreciation group.
Play the accordion.
Organise two fund raising events for 'Help the Aged' every year.
Am interested in compiling histories of local people.

Additional information
I like driving, travelling and visiting historic sites around the country. I enjoy working with people, helping people to learn and am good at organising events.

Keeping records: Handout 4

Curriculum Vitae

Personal Details

Name:

Address:

Telephone No: E-mail address:

Date of birth:

Education and training

Dates	Schools	Qualifications

Employment

Dates	Employer	Job Title	Responsibilities and duties

Voluntary activities

Dates	Organisations	Job title	Responsibilities and duties

Interests

Additional information

Keeping records: Handout 5

My strengths and skills

I can do the following things:

Things I like doing are:

Things I am really good at are:

Understanding Yourself

- What am I like?
- What am I capable of?
- Exploring my life themes
- How I appear to other people

What am I like?

Aims

- To reflect on how life is now.
- To show what life will be like if the current path is followed.
- To decide alternative and more satisfying outcomes.

Preparation

Have available copies of the handout and a whiteboard or flipchart.

Introduction (10 minutes)

Explain the aims for the session. State that most of us get on with life living it from day to day. However, your feelings may be giving you indications that all is not well but you are ignoring the warning, hoping it will go away. It pays to stop every now and then, pay attention and ask: 'How am I feeling?', 'Why am I feeling like this?' Sometimes this is because how we are, is not how we want to be.

Ask the participants to call out words which express how they feel and write them up on the flipchart or board. Examples might be:

Sad	Deceitful	Joyful	Caring
Helpless	Loved	Lonely	Dissatisfied
Selfish	Strong	Incompetent	Abandoned
Anxious	Capable	Disappointed	Hopeless
Guilty	Lazy	Foolish	Bullied
Resentful	Happy	Stupid	Disliked
Jealous	Bad person	Treacherous	Cared for
Angry	Confident	Isolated	Defeated

Activity (20 minutes)

Give out Handout 1 and ask individuals to complete the 'How I feel inside' section by writing down words which describes how they generally feel inside on a regular basis.

When completed, ask them to think about and complete, in they same way, the 'How I present myself' section. This should indicate how they present themselves to the world on a daily basis, which may be quite different to how they feel inside.

Now instruct participants to imagine that they have died and are listening to a group of their friends and family who are talking about them. If they continue living their life in the way that they do now, what do they think their friends would be saying about them? Suggest they consider what people would be saying, taking into account:

- What participants cared about.
- What they stood for.
- The sort of person they were.

They write this down in the 'What my friends will say when I die' section.

Next ask them to think about what they would like their friends to be saying about them. Again ask them to consider what they would be saying, taking into account:

- What they cared about
- What they stood for
- The sort of person they were

After a few moments thought participants write this in the section 'What I would like my friends to say when I die'.

Activity (15 minutes)

Now have participants work in pairs to discuss and share ideas about what they would need to change to achieve the epitaph they want and what they can do to make the changes.

Closure (10 minutes)

Bring the group back together and ask each person to share one thing they have learned about themselves during the session and one thing they could do to become the person they want to be.

Homework (5 minutes)

Instruct participants to carry out at least one thing they could do to become the person they want to be. Discuss any difficulties they think they may encounter and ways they could overcome them.

What am I like? Handout 1

How I feel inside:

How I present myself:

What my friends will say when I die:

What I would like my friends to say when I die:

What I can do to make changes:

What I need to change:

What am I capable of?

Introduction (15 minutes)

Discuss the aims for the session. Draw three columns on the board or flipchart and label each column as shown in the example below. Invite a group member to share something they have achieved in the past. This can be something small, big, work related or personal. Write this in the 'What I achieved' column. Now ask participants what qualities and skills that person needed to achieve this. Write these in the appropriate column. Finally, ask what else might these qualities and skills help that person achieve and write the suggestions on the board. An example is:

What I achieved is:	The qualities and skills this needed were:	Other things these qualities and skills could help me achieve are:
Got a job as a volunteer driver	Determination Courage Research skills Interview skills Ability to drive Enthusiasm	Get a paid job Get a good reference Do a course to learn a new skill Go on a touring holiday Teach my son to drive

Activity (15 minutes)

Give out Handout 1 and ask participants to write down five things they have achieved so far in life. These can be small or big things. Something they did as a teenager or later in life. Once they have written down their achievements, pair people up with a partner. Working together they work out the qualities and skills needed for their achievement and what else these qualities and skills would help them achieve.

Activity (15 minutes)

Give out Handout 2. Individuals now decide on one thing they want to do from all the things they could do and write this down on the handout. Next they note down the skills and qualities they have to achieve this. They then choose a different partner and support each other to work out a step-by-step plan to achieve their goals.

Closure (10 minutes)

Give out some small plain cards or pieces of paper. Ask participants to write their name on the card and one thing they have discovered they are capable of and what they have decided they want to do. The cards or pieces of paper are then put in a bag or hat. Invite group members, one at a time, to pick a card and read out what is written on it.

Homework (5 minutes)

Briefly discuss how individuals will achieve their goals and any barriers or difficulties they may encounter. Have group members suggest any necessary solutions and instruct everyone to carry out their plans.

What am I capable of? Handout 1

What I achieved is:	The qualities and skills this needed were:	Other things these qualities and skills could help me achieve are:
1		
2		
3		
4		
5		

© Robin Dynes. *Instant Session Plans for Essential Life Skills: Learning and Development.* www.russellhouse.co.uk

What am I capable of? Handout 2

What I have decided to do is:

The skills and qualities I have to help me achieve this are:

My plan is:

Step 1:

Step 2:

Step 3:

Step 4:

Step 5:

Exploring my life themes

Aims

- To explore individual life themes.
- To discover personal talents.
- To plan to make use of talents.

Preparation

Have available copies of the handout and a whiteboard or flipchart. (**Note:** Alter the handout to suit the ages of group members. For example, if everyone in the group is less than 30 years old, do not include ages over that.)

Introduction (10 minutes)

Explain the aims for the session. State that everyone has themes that run through their lives. These themes may involve things like helping others, shopping, climbing, computing, collecting, designing things, organising things, negotiating, crafts or writing. What we are happiest doing and most motivated to do usually come out of these themes. It is not always what we are best at but what we most enjoy. Once we know what our themes are we can build skills in that area so we can do what gives us most satisfaction. Ask participants if they can think of themes that run through people's lives and write them up on the board or flipchart. Suggest they think about famous people such as David Beckham as well as their families and friends.

Activity (15 minutes)

Divide the group into pairs. Each pair has a discussion about things they have had aspirations or urges to do and writes them down. It does not matter how far out or fanciful they seem. These can usually be identified by thinking of times in life when they have used expressions like:

'I could do that . . .'

'I wish I had learned more about . . .'

'I'd love to . . .'

'If I had time I would . . .'

'I love . . .'

'If only I could . . .'

'I always wanted to . . .'

Allow a few minutes for discussion and then, back in one group, ask participants to state what their partners' aspirations past and present are.

Activity (15 minutes)

Give out Handout 1. Participants think about things they have enjoyed doing so far during their life at different ages. This might include football, helping people, shopping, travelling, negotiating, looking after a child, etc. Using information from the previous activity and looking back on what they have listed they enjoyed doing they then state what they feel are their life themes. There may be one that stands out or there may be two or three.

Activity (10 minutes)

Participants get together with their previous partner and discuss various ways in which they can use this knowledge to plan what they want to do in the future. Choices might include:

- Obtaining a job where they can use the talent or interest.
- Pursuing it as a hobby.
- Taking a training course to improve skills or get a qualification.

Remind people that they should not set themselves impossible tasks. For example, football might be a theme but they are not particularly good at football. But this would not stop them getting a job in that industry, perhaps training young people to play or working in some role for a local football club. If they enjoyed DIY choices might include:

- Designing kitchens.
- Working for a builder.
- Setting up a DIY service such as decorating or plumbing.
- Working for a furniture company.
- Working for a company offering a DIY service.

Closure (5 minutes)

Invite participants to share what they have discovered as ambitions and themes in their lives and ideas about how they can use these in the future. Encourage group members to make additional suggestions to those already thought up by individuals.

Homework (5 minutes)

To discover more about themselves and the things they enjoy, ask participants to keep a journal. At the end of each day they spend about five minutes reflecting on the events of the day and writing down anything they enjoyed. This might be a particular task like a reception duty, writing a report, organising something, showing someone how to do something, playing a sport, painting a picture, writing a poem or doing the shopping for an elderly neighbour. Suggest they record what it was they particularly enjoyed about doing it. How did they feel while doing it and afterwards? They need to do this for at least a week but preferably about a month to allow theme ideas about what they enjoy doing to fully emerge and to give choices for what they would like to do in the future.

Exploring my life themes: Handout 1

Age	Things I have enjoyed doing are:
1–12	
12–20	
20–30	
30–40	
40–50	
50–60	

My aspirations are:

My life themes are:

Using these themes I could:

How I appear to other people

Aims

- To explore personal impact on other people.
- To discover what needs to change to have a positive impact.
- To retain a sense of perspective on life.

Preparation

Have available copies of the handout and a whiteboard or flipchart.

Introduction (10 minutes)

Explain the aims for the session. Ask: 'What might people say about someone who always looks inwards, is continually focussed on themselves and their own personal needs? What happens to them?' Write the suggestions on the whiteboard or flipchart. This should include:

- They are selfish.
- Self-centred.
- Small things seem big.
- Can become isolated.
- Lose friends.
- They lose a sense of proportion about unimportant things that happen.
- They lose a sense of perspective on life.

Now ask: 'What happens when someone spends time focussing on other people and their needs?' This should include:

- Build friendships.
- Get support from others.
- A good feeling.
- Others like you.
- Helps keep your own life in perspective.
- Helps keep unimportant things in proportion.

Activity (20 minutes)

Have everyone sit in a circle. Ensure there is one empty chair in the circle. Invite one group member to sit in the empty chair. The other group members now take it in turns to state something that person did (in the past or present) and what impact this had on them. Each participant takes a turn in the empty chair.

Examples might be:

Action	Impact
Avoided eye contact every time I looked at him.	Made me wary of approaching him.
Greeted me with a smile, introduced himself and asked me how I got here.	I immediately felt comfortable talking to him.
Told me all about himself. Never once asked how I was.	Thought he was only interested in himself. Couldn't care less about me.
Helped me plan how to do my homework.	I felt good and that I had made a friend.
He looked sad and thoughtful.	I wondered if something had happened to upset him. Did not know whether or not to speak to him. Decided not to.

Activity (15 minutes)

Give out Handout 1. Instruct participants to write down names of their immediate family, friends, colleagues and others and complete the handout except for the 'I will change this by' section. Suggest that it is best to concentrate initially on two or three people with whom they do not have a particularly good relationship.

Closure (10 minutes)

Invite each person, in turn, to state one 'impact' they would like to change and what impact they would like to have instead. The other group members make suggestions about how this could be achieved. Each person then writes down their chosen action to make the change.

Homework (5 minutes)

Suggest that individuals check out the impact they think they have with the individuals concerned – sometimes the impact can be different to that thought and requires a different remedy. Hold a brief discussion on difficulties that may be encountered carrying out chosen actions and instruct participants to complete them.

How I appear to other people: Handout 1

Impact on	Action (What I do)	The impact my behaviour has is:	The impact I would like to have is:
Family			
Friends			
Colleagues			
Others			

The impact I would like to change is:

I will change this by:

Learning From Experience

- Learning from life events
- A day in the life
- The power of feedback
- Tuning in to values

Learning from life events

Aims

- To focus on a few important life events.
- To reflect on what can be learned from them.
- To understand the learning cycle.

Preparation

Have available copies of the handouts and a whiteboard or flipchart.

Introduction (5 minutes)

Discuss the aims for the session. State that events that happen to us – both good and bad – are opportunities to learn. What we decide to do in the future is influenced by past experiences. Therefore it is important that we reflect on what has happened to avoid bad experiences being repeated and to build on good experiences.

Activity (10 minutes)

Give out Handout 1 and ask participants to think back on experiences from their life as a child up to the present day. Suggest that they choose three good events and three events which were not so good. These could be events like:

- Leaving home
- Losing a job
- Getting into debt
- Not passing an exam
- Getting a promotion
- Birth of son

Activity (15 minutes)

Split the group members into pairs. Participants then share one of their experiences and what they learned from it. Instruct partners to help each other by asking questions such as:

- What happened?
- What was the outcome?
- Why do you think that happened?
- What did you do?
- If it happened again how would you ensure a different outcome?
- How could you avoid this in the future?

End the activity – back as group – by inviting volunteers to share with everyone what they learned from their experience.

Activity (5 minutes)

Give out Handout 2. Explain that the process everyone has gone through is known as 'The Learning Cycle'. It has four steps. These are:

1. An event happens.
2. The person later reflects on that experience – thinks about it and, perhaps, discusses it with other people.
3. Learns something from what has occurred.
4. Plans future steps – how to handle it in the future or avoid it happening again.

Activity (10 minutes)

Give out Handout 3. Individuals pair up with someone different, discuss another life event, what they learned from it and their plan for the future. They record their findings on the handout.

Closure (10 minutes)

Re-form as a group and ask participants what other events in life they think they could use this process to learn from. Write suggestions on the whiteboard. This may include:

- An interview for a job.
- Asking a girlfriend out.
- An accident.
- Doing an exam.
- Going on holiday.
- Buying a car.
- Sharing a flat.
- Applying for a training course.

End the activity by inviting members, in turn, to state something they have learned from the session.

Homework (5 minutes)

Instruct participants to practice using the process for other events in their lives and record the outcome on Handout 3.

Learning from life events: Handout 1

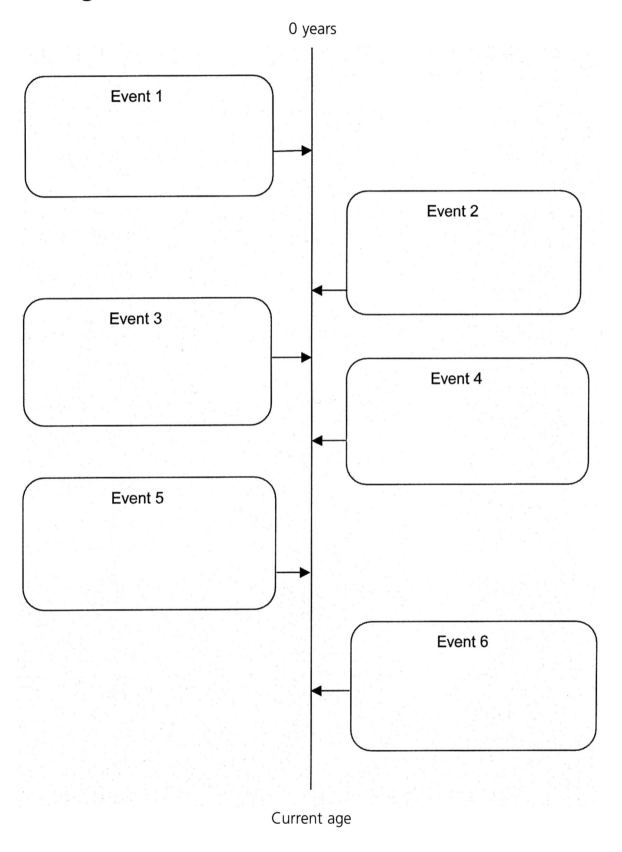

0 years

Event 1

Event 2

Event 3

Event 4

Event 5

Event 6

Current age

Learning from life events: Handout 2

The Learning Cycle

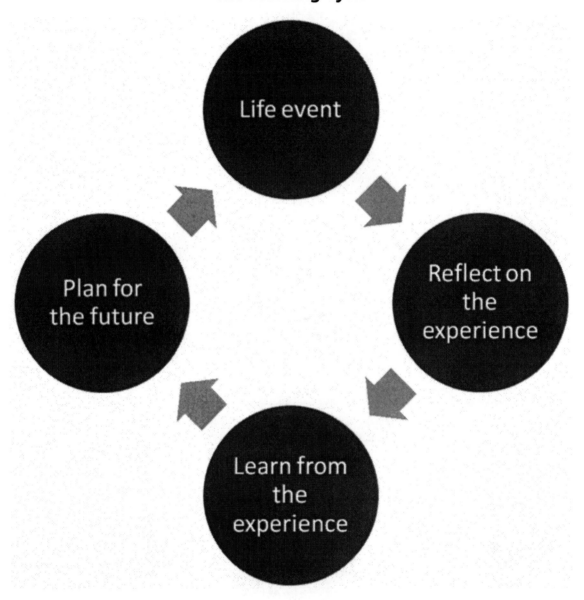

Learning from life events: Handout 3

Life event	Reflections about the event	What I learned from it	My plan for the future

A day in the life

Aims

- To reflect and learn from a typical day.
- To examine the skills used in a day.
- To discover what you do well and could develop further.

Preparation

Have available copies of the handouts and a whiteboard or flipchart.

Introduction (10 minutes)

Explain the aims for the session. State that the session will show what can be learned from examining a day in their life. Invite participants, in turn, to state briefly what their day so far has been like.

Activity (30 minutes)

Give out Handout 1.

Stage 1: Ask participants to choose a typical day in their life. They write down the main things they did since getting up, recording the time, what they did, who else was involved and a comment on what they did as shown in the examples below.

Time	What I did	Who else was involved	Comment	Skills I used
7:40	Got up and did some exercises.	No one	Keeps me healthy and fit.	Discipline and timekeeping
8:00	Had breakfast with flatmate.	Flat mate	Discussed what we will do after work.	Decision making Listening and expressing opinion
8:15	Went to work.	No one	Boring.	Driving
8:30	Made some phone calls to customers.	Customers	Enjoyed chatting to them.	Communication skills Negotiating Planning

| 8:45 | Had meeting with my manager. | Manager | Enjoy meetings to plan weekly schedules. | Negotiating Decision making Expressing opinion Providing information and data |
| 9:15 | Stopped at mini-market on way to first customer. | Shop assistant | Liked chatting to him about what to buy. | Decision making Research Communication skills |

Stage 2: Ask for an example from the 'What I did' column recorded by participants and examine the skills the person needed to do it. Write these up on the whiteboard or flipchart. Do at least two or three examples.

Stage 3:

Divide the group into pairs. Partners now help each other record the skills needed to do what they have recorded and write these on their handouts.

Stage 4:

Instruct participants to summarise the main skills they have used during their typical day and select from this the things that they feel they do well.

Activity (5 minutes)

Invite participants to state skills they have discovered they possess and feel they are good at.

Closure (10 minutes)

Facilitate a short discussion, asking the following:

Is anyone surprised at the range of skills they use on a day-to-day basis?

Are any of these skills transferable into other situations/tasks? Which? Ask for examples.

Have any patterns emerged in the skills people use or enjoy? For example: a preference for people orientated tasks, being creative, working with data and information, organising and planning things, working with things and so on. Ask for examples.

Homework (5 minutes)

Instruct participants to carry out the above exercise on several different days to explore more fully their range of skills and what they do well and enjoy doing. They can then use Handout 2 to choose which skills they might like to develop in the future.

A day in the life: Handout 1

Time	What I did	Who else was involved	Comment	Skills I used

The main skills I have used today are:

Things I do well and like doing are:

A day in the life: Handout 2

Skills I enjoy using	Other situations I can use these skills in	Skills I would like to develop

The power of feedback

Aims

- To explore the value of feedback.
- To examine strategies to learn from feedback.
- To practice receiving feedback.

Preparation

Have available copies of Handout 1 and the cut-outs from Handout 2.

Introduction (10 minutes)

Go through the aims for the session. Explain that feedback is the information we are given by someone else in response to a task we have completed, a choice we have made, a behaviour or something we have done. They might say what a good job we have done, how we could have improved on it, or that it was a bad decision. This information may or may not be given in a constructive and helpful way and may be either positive or negative or a combination of both.

Instruct participants to think back to when they have had feedback from a teacher, a manager, a parent, a friend or a colleague. How did they feel when being given the information? Embarrassed? Angry? Anxious? Grateful? Invite each person, in turn, to state how they felt at the time. Ask:

- How did they react? Did they block the feedback by denial, defending themselves, attacking or avoiding?
- Are any of these helpful ways to react to feedback? Why not? What benefits are there from getting feedback?

Activity (15 minutes)

Give out Handout 1. Go through and discuss each step of the strategy outlined with the group.

Activity (20 minutes)

Split the participants into sub-groups of three people. Instruct each person in the sub-groups to take turns in giving and receiving feedback to another member of the sub-group. While they are doing that the third member of the group can act as a prompter to help the person receiving feedback of the stages as they occur. Give each person one of the situations cut out from Handout 2. This is the situation that they will receive feedback on. Alternatively, you can compile situations appropriate to your participants to use.

Closure (10 minutes)

Ask and discuss the following:

- What is your reaction when offered feedback?
- What is the point of being objective about feedback and seeing it as feedback on the task, behaviour etc. and not of you?
- What is the value of listening, clarifying and evaluating information offered?
- Do they think following a strategy like this will enable them to make a good decision? Why?

Finally, emphasise that these skills take both time and practice to acquire and feel comfortable while carrying them out.

Homework (5 minutes)

Instruct participants to practice the skill by asking someone to give them feedback. This could be a parent, a manager, a teacher, a colleague or a friend and may be for a task completed, a behaviour, an attitude, a skill, a report they have written or on something they want to do.

The power of feedback: Handout 1

Step 1: Adopt a positive attitude

- Acknowledge the usefulness of feedback.
- Recognise when someone is preparing to give you feedback. ('I want to talk to you.' 'We need to talk.')
- Be aware of your body language. Take a deep breath and breathe out letting go of any tension.
- Use positive self-talk. ('I can learn from this.' 'This could be really useful.')
- Be prepared to listen and consider what is being said. (You might not like it but you can evaluate it later. And, don't make the assumption that all feedback is damning. Feedback includes telling you what is good.)
- When you think it will be useful, ask for feedback.
- Remember, although sometimes the words may sound accusing, it is the behaviour or how you did the task that is being discussed, not you.

Step 2: Listen and clarify

- Check your understanding of what behaviour or action is being discussed
- What evidence is being presented?
- What changes are being requested?
- Ask questions to clarify anything you do not understand.
- Restate your understanding of the feedback.

Step 3: Evaluate

- How accurate is the evidence?
- What is the experience/qualification of the person giving feedback?
- Have other people given me similar feedback?
- How relevant is this to me?

Step 4: Make a decision

- What will I lose or gain by making any change?
- Would a compromise provide a solution?
- Will the changes work?
- Am I willing to make the changes?

The power of feedback: Handout 2

An employee receiving feedback from their manager on performance.

A worker receiving feedback from a colleague about their attitude.

A spouse receiving feedback from their partner on their lack of support with the children.

A group member receiving feedback from another member on their contribution in the group.

A person receiving feedback on a job they have done for a neighbour.

A person receiving feedback from their partner on how they treat their friends.

A child receiving feedback from their parent on their choice of clothes.

A parent receiving feedback from their child about their discriminating attitude.

A child receiving feedback from their parent on their cooking skills.

A tenant receiving feedback from their landlord on how they look after the property.

Tuning in to values

Aims

- To reflect on personal values.
- To consider how values affect decisions.
- To explore how they affect current decisions to be made.

Preparation

Have available copies of the handouts and a whiteboard or flipchart.

Introduction (10 minutes)

Go through the aims for the sessions. Explain that being happy in life involves knowing what really matters to us. We often refer to these as 'values'. These values make us what we are and determine what decisions we make and what actions we take in life. When we are true to these values life is good and we feel happy.

Examples of values might be:

- Honesty
- Being on time
- Peace of mind
- Staying healthy
- Being creative
- Having fun
- Shared values
- Time with friends
- Contributing to the community

- Status
- Doing work that is challenging
- Being valued for skills
- Respect
- Security
- Money
- Reducing pollution
- Sense of humour
- Being loved

Ask participants to think of some others and write them up on the whiteboard.

When completed state that some values have been with us from childhood. These have been acquired through family, education, cultural background and peer groups etc. Sometimes we are not aware we have them and they only come to our attention when we feel unhappy about something. Becoming aware of our values can help us understand what is holding us back and help us choose how we want to behave in any situation.

Activity (15 minutes)

Stage 1

Give out Handout 1. Ask each person to record in the different areas what is important to them.

Stage 2

Instruct participants to write down three decisions they have made in the past. This could be:

- To move house.
- To do voluntary work.
- To change a job.
- To break off a relationship.

They then reflect on this decision and write down if and how this decision was influenced by their values.

Activity (10 minutes)

Facilitate a discussion on the findings from the previous activity. Encourage participants to share what they have learned about their values and how these have influenced their decisions.

Activity (10 minutes)

Give out Handout 2. Participants list their values under the headings provided. They then answer the question 'Is this value being dishonoured at present?' and state how this is affecting them at present. Finally, they decide what action, if any, they need to take.

Closure (10 minutes)

Facilitate a discussion on what participants have discovered about their values, how they affect how they currently feel and decisions or actions they need to consider at present.

Point out that our values change as we progress through life and need to be revisited from time to time. If we are feeling unhappy about something then a value may have changed.

Homework (5 minutes)

Instruct participants to choose a decision or action that needs to be considered and do something to work towards bringing it into line with the value it dishonours. Suggest they record in a diary how they feel after taking the action.

Tuning in to values: Handout 1

Personal	Work

Relationships	Community/Social

Three decisions I have made in the past are:	How this decision was influenced by my values is:
1	
2	
3	

Tuning in to values: Handout 2

Values	How these are affecting me at present is:	Decisions/actions I need to consider are:
Personal		
Work		
Relationships		
Community/social		

Planning for Your Future

- What I really, really want
- Stepping stones to successful planning
- Making it happen
- Overcoming obstacles to achievement

What I really, really want

Aims

- To identify long and short term goals.
- To provide some direction in life.
- To build motivation to take action.

Preparation

Have available copies of the handouts and a whiteboard or flipchart.

Introduction (10 minutes)

Go through the aims for the session. Give out some slips of paper and ask each participant to write down something they really wanted to do or achieve when they were a child or a teenager. This might have been to go somewhere, wanting to do a particular job or to buy something. It does not matter if they achieved it or not. When this has been completed collect them and place them in a bag or other receptacle. Now have individuals pick one out at random. If anyone gets their own back they must not say so but act like it belongs to someone else. Next invite group members, in turn, to read out what is written on the piece of paper they are holding. The other participants try to guess who wrote it.

When the process has been completed state that the process they have just completed is very similar to the beginning stage of setting long and short term goals. You think of things that you really, really want to do or achieve.

Activity (10 minutes)

Give out Handout 1. Ask participants to imagine themselves in 5 or 10 years time. What would they like to be doing at work, in their personal life, socially or any other sphere of life? Instruct them to think for a few minutes and then either write or draw what they really, really want. Perhaps they see themselves working as a photographer, with a young family, taking part in a local dramatic society as an amateur actor, managing their department at work or travelling. What they want needs to:

- Be specific so they can see themselves doing it.
- Be realistic.
- Mean something to them.

Activity (10 minutes)

Give out Handout 2. Participants choose a priority goal from all they have written down and then pair up with a partner to discuss what steps they could take during the next twelve months towards achieving it. They write their steps on the handout and when they will be able to achieve them.

Activity (5 minutes)

Instruct participants to change partners. This time partners question each other and discuss how realistic and achievable their goals are for the year and make any necessary adjustments.

Activity (10 minutes)

Participants change partners again. This time they discuss what motivates them to achieve what they want. Are they motivated by money, status, the challenge, the creativity involved, the respect this will earn them, to be loved, the satisfaction from helping other people, etc? They then write their conclusions down on Handout 2.

Closure (10 minutes)

Write the following statement beginnings on the whiteboard or flipchart and invite each person to complete the statements:

- What I really, really want in ten years is . . .
- My goal for the next twelve months is . . .
- My motivation is . . .

Homework (5 minutes)

Suggest that participants revisit their ambition for the ten years and their goals for the next year to check it is what they really, really want. When they have done so they then, on a daily basis, spend a short time:

- Relaxing. They might do a relaxation exercise or listen to some relaxing music.
- They then, for a few minutes: visualise themselves in ten years time carrying out their ambition.
- Finally, they visualise themselves in 12 months time and how they will feel when they have taken some positive steps towards achieving that ambition.

What I really, really want: Handout 1

What I really, really want: Handout 2

What I want to be doing in 10 years time is:

My goal for the next 12 months is:

Goal

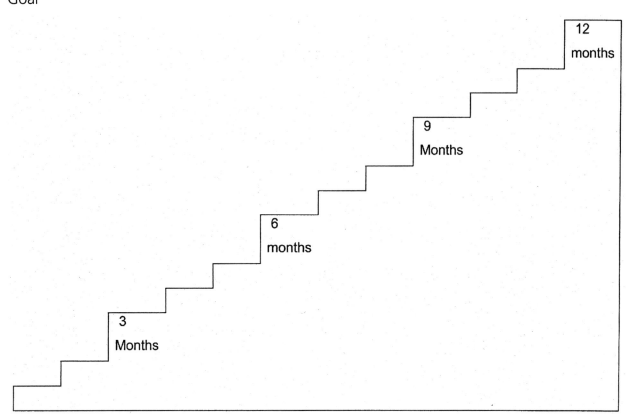

My motivation for achieving this is:

1.

2.

3.

Stepping stones to successful planning

Aims

- To provide a framework for gathering information.
- To consider the information needed to draw up an action plan.
- To practice using the process.

Preparation

Have available copies of the handouts and a whiteboard or flipchart.

Introduction (20 minutes)

Explain the aims for the session. State that when a goal has been decided on the first step is to gain enough information and knowledge to be able to plan a course of action that will succeed.

Give out Handout 1 and also draw it on a whiteboard or flipchart. Discuss each step of the information gathering process. Have a suitable goal in mind to demonstrate the process and encourage participants to call out examples for each step as they are discussed. Write these up on the board.

Activity (20 minutes)

Divide the participants into two subgroups. Give out Handout 2 and some flipchart sheets. Instruct each group to work on the case study outlined in the handout or use a case study you have created yourself more suitable to the group member situations.

Activity (10 minutes)

Instruct the subgroups to present their findings. One group will likely contribute information that the other group has not considered.

Closure (5 minutes)

Ask participants to think of a goal that they have failed to achieve in the past or did not work as well as expected. Which of the information gathering steps needed strengthening or did they leave out before doing their action planning?

Homework (5 minutes)

Give out Handout 3 and instruct participants to apply the exercise to a goal they have set themselves to achieve in the future. This may be a goal from the 'What I really, really want' session.

Stepping stones to successful planning: Handout 1

Stepping stones to successful planning: Handout 2

Case study

Jane has two children who are now growing up. Her son has started attending college and her daughter has got a job training to be a hairdresser. Jane has had some mental ill health in the past. A few years earlier she was forced to give up a part time job she had because of the stress looking after the two children combined with working. For the past two years, to supplement household income, she has provided accommodation for two foreign students who have been learning to speak English. She has really enjoyed helping them with their assignments. She now wants to become a tutor teaching foreign students who want to learn English.

She is aware that her own standard of English is probably not good enough for her to do a teacher training course immediately. But, she is very keen to do this as she feels it will boost her confidence, she will really enjoy doing it and it will provide extra income for the household.

She knows that her husband is not keen on her going out to work again as he fears that she might become stressed and have another breakdown. She feels guilty because of all the extra hours her husband has had to work over the years to support the family.

Stepping stones to successful planning: Handout 3

What is my goal?

What is my motivation for doing this?

Who will support me?

Where can I get information, advice and guidance?

What skills and knowledge do I need?

How can I acquire the skills I need to succeed?

What is my plan to obtain the information I need?	When am I going to complete each step?
1	
2	
3	
4	
5	
6	

Making it happen

Aims

- To understand how to develop an action plan
- To gather all the necessary information together
- To prepare an action plan

Preparation

Have available copies of the handouts, envelopes and some sheets of paper to write on. It is ideal if participants have completed the sessions on 'What I really, really want' or another session in which they have explored goals they want to achieve in the next twelve months and 'Stepping stones to successful planning'. This will ensure they have all the information they need to complete the activities in this session.

Introduction (10 minutes)

Go through the aims for the session. Invite each group member, in turn, to state a strength they have or something that they are good at which will help them achieve any goals they set themselves. Statements might include: I am determined, I am good at organising, I have strong motivation, I am a good listener, I am good at planning, I am good at coming up with ideas, I am good at completing things I have started, I am good at learning from my mistakes, I am good at asking for help when needed, I am good at negotiating, I am good at collecting information, I am good at improvising when things go wrong and so on. See if you can go round the group two or three times with people stating strengths or things they are good at doing.

Activity (35 minutes)

Give out Handout 1 and 2 and instruct participants to work on their personal action plan, completing Handout 1 first. State that as action plans may cover areas which are considered private some people might prefer to work on their own to prepare it. Others might like to work in pairs to share ideas. Make it clear that even if they work on their own they can still ask for advice or ideas when they need it.

Closure (10 minutes)

Give each person an envelope and a sheet of paper. Instruct them to write a brief letter to themselves stating what they hope to achieve by their first review date. They place their letter in the envelope, address it to themselves and write the review date on the back. Collect the envelopes and keep. Post them two days before the chosen review dates.

Homework (5 minutes)

Briefly discuss any problems individuals have had completing their plans. Instruct them to finish any plans not fully completed and to draw up another action plan for a goal in a different area of life to the one completed. Warn participants not to complete plans for too many goals as taking on too much may prove to be self-defeating.

Making it happen: Handout 1

What I want to achieve over the next twelve months is:

Work:

Personal life:

Social life:

Other:

My priority goal is:

What I need to do to achieve this is: (*List all the actions you need to take. Do not worry about sequence. After completing the list, number them according to which comes first.*)

Making it happen: Handout 2

Actions I need to take (*in sequence*)	Who will support me?	Start date	Completion date

I will review my progress and make necessary adjustments to my plan on: (*List dates*)

1

2

3

4

Overcoming obstacles to achievement

Aims

- To examine a method of overcoming difficulties in the way of achievement.
- To identify what helps and what hinders achievement.
- To maximise what helps and minimise what hinders.

Preparation

Have available copies of the handouts and a whiteboard or flipchart. You might like to substitute the case study in Handout 2 with a situation that is a better fit with the circumstances of the group members.

Introduction (5 minutes)

Explain the aims for the session. Ask participants if, when they have set a goal for the future, they expect everything to be plain sailing or if there are likely to be obstacles to be overcome in order to achieve what they want. State that this session is about looking at a method of anticipating, planning to overcome them and avoiding becoming de-motivated or giving up on the goal.

Activity (20 minutes)

Give out Handout 1 or an alternative you have thought up that is more suited to the group needs and allow a few minutes for people to read through it. At the top of the whiteboard or flipchart write down what is John's goal. Underneath, draw a dividing line down the centre of the whiteboard. Head one side 'What will help? and the other side 'What will hinder?' (similar to the layout shown in Handout 2)

Now have participants call out what they think will help him achieve his goal and what might hinder him. Write these on the board under the appropriate heading.

When this has been completed ask:

- What could be done to maximise the helping factors? (For example, John may be able to negotiate some study time allowance with his line manager who is supportive.)
- What could be done to minimise the hindering factors? (For example, his mother or mother in law may be able to look after the children for short periods to help relieve the stress on his wife.)

Write all the ideas up on the whiteboard or a flipchart (Use the headings shown in Handout 2) and then as a group evaluate all the ideas and how they could be used to strengthen the helping factors and lessen the hindering factors.

Activity (10 minutes)

Give out Handout 2. Individuals think of a goal they want to achieve. (This might be the goal decided on from the 'What I really, really want' session.) They then write down on the handout all the things that will help and anything that might hinder them.

Activity (10 minutes)

Now in pairs have them discuss how they can strengthen the helps and minimise what is listed as hinders. They write down all their ideas and decide which ones they can use.

Closure (10 minutes)

Discuss as a group:

- What benefits are there to looking at helps and hinders in this way?
- Are there benefits to sharing and discussing the issues with other people?
- How do they feel about their goal now they have gone though this process? Does it seem more achievable?

Homework (5 minutes)

Suggest participants try the process out with another goal they have set. This might be:

- With the family
- At work
- Socially
- Other

Overcoming obstacles to achievement: Handout 1

Case study

John wants to obtain a management qualification so he can get promotion at work and earn more money to support his young family. The course will take about one year to complete.

He has some limited experience of managing a few projects and has the support of his line manager.

He is concerned about money. He has to work lots of overtime in order to boost the family income enough to meet all the bills. His wife works part time and looks after their two young children but because she has had some ill health she finds this exhausting. She does however, think, it would be a good thing for John to do and would be a positive move for their future but is unsure about how they will cope for the year.

John will have to do the course in the evening. It will also mean he will have to take on extra responsibility at work to show he can apply the learning and be able to provide some of the evidence he needs to gain the qualification.

John welcomes the extra responsibility but fears that doing the course will put extra stress on his wife and he will be able to spend less time with the children to support her.

Overcoming obstacles to achievement: Handout 2

My goal is:

What will help me achieve this is:	What will hinder me achieving this is:

Actions I can take to maximise the helping factors are:	Actions I can take to minimise the hindering factors are:

End Session for Essential Life Skills

Aims

- To evaluate progress and the course.
- To identify future development.
- To explore methods of maintaining progress.
- To say goodbye.

Preparation

Prepare copies of the handout and have available a flipchart or board to write on, three loose flipchart sheets and some magic markers.

Introduction (5 minutes)

Explain the aims for the session. State that as this is the last session it is important to:

- Review progress
- Ensure everyone has a plan to continue their development in the future
- Evaluate what has gone well and not so well so that improvements can be made to any subsequent courses

Activity (15 minutes)

Give out Handout 1 and ask participants to rate themselves. When completed, give back the rating charts they competed at the beginning of the course. Ask:

- Has there been any improvement in any of the areas rated?
- What areas do they need to continue to strengthen?

Briefly discuss the findings and ask participants to record this in the spaces provided. For the moment they can leave the 'I will do this by . . .' section blank.

Activity (15 minutes)

Facilitate a quick brainstorming session on ways in which they can maintain and develop their skills. Write the suggestions on a flipchart or board. When completed invite participants to complete the 'I will do this by . . .' section of Handout 1.

Activity (10 minutes)

Place a flipchart sheet on three separate tables with magic markers. Head one 'What went well?'; the second 'What could be improved?' and the third 'Rate your facilitator (1–10)'.

Inform the group that you will leave the room for 10 minutes and ask each person to write something on each sheet during that time.

When you return, collect the flipchart sheets, thank the group for their input and give an opportunity for any further comments.

Activity (5 minutes)

Produce the flipchart sheets you used in Session 1, recording the aim for the course and individual expectations. Go through the expectations one-by-one and ask if group members feel they have been achieved. Tick them off as you go. Now ask if they feel the overall aim of the course has also been achieved.

Closure (10 minutes)

Thank everyone and congratulate them on their achievement on completing the course. Remind them of the importance of carrying out their plan to continue their development. Finally, invite everyone to circulate, congratulate each other, say something personal to each other like 'I have enjoyed your company', 'Thank you for your support' or 'When I was feeling down you made me smile', shake hands and say farewell.

End session for Essential Life Skills: Handout 1

Self-rating chart

Name: _____ Date: _____

Rate your ability in the following areas:	Poor				Good
	1	2	3	4	5
	1	2	3	4	5
	1	2	3	4	5
	1	2	3	4	5
	1	2	3	4	5
	1	2	3	4	5
	1	2	3	4	5
	1	2	3	4	5
	1	2	3	4	5
	1	2	3	4	5

I have improved in the following areas:

_____

Areas I need to strengthen are:

_____

I will achieve this by:

_____

Alphabetic list of Sessions

A
Active motivating strategies
A day in the life

C
Changing your attitude
Creating a vision
Creative thinking

D
Don't live with it: improve it!

E
Emotional health and self-development
through writing
Exploring my life themes

H
How I appear to other people
How I learn

I
Identifying what is important
Increasing positive energy

K
Keeping records

L
Learning from life events
Learning to negotiate

M
Making it happen
Marketing your strengths and skills
Monitoring progress and avoiding inertia

O
Overcoming barriers to learning
Overcoming obstacles to achievement

P
Planning to learn
Promoting your creativity

R
Releasing your creativity
Rules for living

S
Stepping stones to successful planning

T
Taking stock of your skills
The freedom of boundaries
The learning power of questions
The power of feedback
To be a life coach
Tuning in to values

U
Understanding emotions
Using communication styles to change feelings
Using emotional communication skills

W
Watch your language!
What am I capable of?
What am I like?
What I really, really want
What motivates me?
When the going gets tough

Instant Session Plans for Essential Life Skills

By
Robin Dynes

This comprehensive series of four books addresses the essential and acquirable skills we all use to manage and cope with life. The topics covered are:

Self Management
Contents
Assertiveness
Building Confidence
Time Management
Self-esteem
Anger Management
Stress
Daily Living Skills
Managing Change
Self-awareness
Encouraging Creative Thinking

Learning and Development
Contents
Unlocking Your Potential
Learning to Learn
Becoming Self-motivated
Self-coaching
Emotional Development
Harnessing Creativity
Life Management Skills
Understanding Yourself
Learning from Experience
Planning for Your Future

Health and Well-being
Contents
Managing Worries
Looking After Your Mental Health
Coping with Depression
Dealing with a Crisis
Healthy Living
Bereavement and Loss
Staying Positive
Changing Your Habits
Taking Risks
Learning to Relax

Relationships
Contents
Communication Skills
Relationship Skills
Resolving Conflicts
Building a Support Network
Expressing Feelings
Making Friends
Working with Other People
Being Part of a Team
Networking Skills
Interview Skills

Due Autumn 2009

**For more detailed information on these and our other publications, please visit:
www.russellhouse.co.uk**

Electronic supply of the handouts from Instant Session Plans for Essential Life Skills: Learning and Development

If you would like to receive a PDF of the handouts from this book, please complete the form below, tear out this page, and return it to us. Please note that photocopies are not acceptable, nor are applications made through e-mail, phone or fax.

Please keep a copy of the completed form for your own records.

This PDF is free.

Please note

RHP reserves the right to withdraw this offer at any time without prior notice.

RHP reserves the right to qualify or reject any application which it is not completely satisfied is on an original torn-out page from the back of a purchased book.

Terms and conditions for use of the handouts from Instant Session Plans for Essential Life Skills: Learning and Development

1. Buying a copy of *Instant Session Plans for Essential Life Skills: Learning and Development* and completing this form gives the individual who signs the form permission to use the materials in the PDF that will be sent from RHP for their own use only.
2. The hard copies that they then print from the PDF are subject to the same permissions and restrictions that are set out in the 'photocopying permission' section at the front of this book.
3. Under no circumstances should they forward or copy the electronic materials to anyone else.
4. If the person who signs this form wants a licence to be granted for wider use of the electronic materials within their organisation, network or client base, they must make a request directly to RHP fully detailing the proposed use. All requests will be reviewed on their own merits.
   - If the request is made when submitting this form to RHP, the request should be made in writing and should accompany this form.
   - If the request is made later, it should be made in an email sent to help@russellhouse.co.uk, and should not only fully detail the proposed use, but also give the details of the person whose name and contact details were on the original application form.

RHP and the author expect this honour system to be followed respectfully, by individuals and organisations whom we in turn respect. RHP will act to protect authors' copyright if they become aware of it being infringed.

I would like to receive a free PDF of the handouts from *Instant Session Plans for Essential Life Skills: Learning and Development*.

*Name _____

*Address _____

_____

_____

_____

*Post code _____

*Contact phone number _____

*e-mail address _____ (to which the PDF will be e-mailed).

I have read, and accept, the terms and conditions. I understand that RHP may use this information to contact me about other matters and publications, but that RHP will not make my details available to other organisations.

*Signed: _____   *Date _____

* All sections marked with an asterisk **must be completed**, or the form will be returned to the postal address given here.

Please return to: Russell House Publishing Ltd, 4 St Georges House, The Business Park,
Uplyme Road, Lyme Regis, Dorset DT7 3LS.